APPEARANCE AND REALITY
The Two Truths in Four Buddhist Systems

APPEARANCE AND REALITY
The Two Truths in Four Buddhist Systems

by

Guy Newland

Snow Lion Publications
Ithaca, New York

Snow Lion Publications
P.O. Box 6483
Ithaca, New York 14851 U.S.A.
Telephone: 607-273-8519

ISBN 1-55939-131-6

Printed in Canada on acid-free recycled paper.

Library of Congress Cataloging-in-Publication Data

Newland, Guy.
     Appearance and reality : the two truths in four Buddhist systems /
by Guy Newland.
             p.   cm.
     Includes bibliographical references
     ISBN 1-55939-131-6 (alk. paper)
     1. Dge-lugs-pa (Sect)--Doctrines. 2. Truth (Buddhism) I. Title.
BQ7640.N47 1999
294.3'420423--DC21   99-25977
                                            CIP

Contents

Introduction

When someone comes to you seeking to understand Buddhism, where should you start? Should you elaborate on what it means to take refuge in the three jewels? Should you analyze the four noble truths, taking a cue from the Buddha's first sermon?

Joshua Cutler (Director of the Tibetan Buddhist Learning Center in Washington, New Jersey) asked the Dalai Lama this question, and the Dalai Lama suggested that for many in the West today, the two truths—conventional truth and ultimate truth—is the best place to start. He argued that it is best to lead people into dharma via exposure to philosophical reasoning and analysis of the nature of reality. Based upon this advice, Joshua organized a seminar, inviting Tibetan and Western scholars to teach about the two truths in the Buddhist systems they knew best. He sent tapes of these talks to me; I listened to them carefully and was inspired by them as I wrote the first draft of this book for use at the center. Others who found value in that draft asked that I publish it.

What is Real?

When the Buddha awoke from the dream we still dream, he saw the ultimate reality of things just as they are. And yet, motivated by concern for our welfare, he worked within the world of conventional appearances, using the conventions of language to point us in the right direction. Buddhist philosophy attempts to clarify the philosophical and intellectual content of this core Buddhist story. It is a story which turns on a perennial human theme: the doubleness of the world. There are shifting appearances and conventions, the manners and traditions of the vast and diverse world; and then there is the mystery of things just as they are, sheer reality. And yet we cannot find this reality anywhere else but right here in the midst of shifting appearances. Buddhist philosophers call this doubleness the two truths, conventional truth and ultimate truth. Each system of Buddhist philosophy has its own way of explaining exactly what these two truths are and how they relate to one another. In exploring these systems, we are looking over the shoulders of Buddhist thinkers as they grapple with a basic question: What is real?

This is not an idle intellectual question, but a matter which cuts to the heart of our practice in life. If clear analysis of reality reveals no substantial, personal self, then who are we anyway? And if analysis of reality reveals no absolutely established moral standards, then how shall we be guided in living with one another? Practice is something that happens in the midst of these tangles, liberating and illuminating us.

"What is real?" is, among other things, a question that demands intellectual analysis. Practice transforms the whole person, including the intellect. In some types of Tibetan Buddhism, including the Dalai Lama's Geluk (*dGe lugs*) tradition, practice includes sharpening the intellect into a sword of discriminating wisdom. Followers of the Geluk tradition insist that wisdom can never be a matter of withdrawing from ignorance and delusion into some kind of spacy, non-conceptual state. If enlightenment were simply a matter of stopping the stream of conceptual thinking, then a hammer blow to the head ought to produce some very profound wisdom![1]

Instead of backing away from the tangles of dualistic thought, we must work to see things as they are, using logic to critique our own misunderstandings. Only when we understand reality well can we begin to refine this wisdom toward the direct and trans-conceptual insight of nirvāna. Thus, for the Dalai Lama and his Geluk tradition, serious study of Buddhist philosophical tenets is not a scholarly sideline to practice—it is vital and fundamental practice. In the *Descent into Laṅkā Sūtra*, the Buddha says:

> My teaching has two modes:
> Advice and tenets.
> To children I give advice,
> And to yogis I give tenets.[2]

Tenet Systems

The structure of the four tenet systems presented here is not derived from the chronological development of these systems in India, and this is true whether you refer to a traditional Tibetan Buddhist chronology or a contemporary Western academic chronology.[3] When you begin your systematic study of Buddhist philosophy with the study of these tenet systems, you are not taking an historical approach. For this reason, some scholars have criticized the use of tenet systems as a conceptual key to Buddhist philosophy. They argue that it blurs distinctions between Indian teachers who may have lived hundreds of years apart. They argue that these "tenet systems" exist much more clearly and distinctly in the imaginations of Tibetans than they did in the lives of the Indian philosophers who are classified by the scheme. They are especially concerned to avoid letting tenet system schemes supercede study of primary sources of our understanding of Buddhist philosophies.

I am sympathetic to these criticisms. Tenet study should not be the end-point of our philosophical explorations; it is not a serious alternative to reading Nāgārjuna and Vasubandhu. On the other hand, I think some Western scholars have gone too far in dismissing Tibetan tenet system literature. Although it is detached from the history of the ideas it presents, it gives us a working framework for thinking about Buddhist philosophies. Underestimating the scholarship that Tibetans like Jamyang Shayba ('Jam dbyangs bzhad pa) put into their analyses of Indian Buddhist philosophy, some scholars have taken years to arrive at conclusions they might otherwise have reached (at least tentatively) in weeks, days, or hours.

Unless our interests are narrowly academic, we cannot care so much about the history of the ideas until we have some good sense of what the ideas are. And tenet system literature is a great place to look for that understanding. If we keep in mind that this particular scheme was created in Tibet as a way to structure a coherent worldview that takes account of the diversity of Indian Buddhist philosophy, we will be using it in a correct and helpful way. I am thankful to the Tibetan scholars who did this work, providing us with the benefit of their perspective.

It should be very clear, therefore, that this book does not attempt to survey Buddhist philosophy, nor even the breadth of Tibetan Buddhist philosophy. I have written for readers who have some familiarity with Buddhism and are genuinely interested in the philosophical aspects of Indian or Tibetan Buddhism, but who may feel daunted by scholarly translations of very technical material. What I present here—key ideas from four systems according to the traditional interpretation of the Geluk order—can be, I hope, a bridge, or at least a stepping-stone, to wider understanding and deeper questioning.

Acknowledgements

In this book, I share things I have heard from many Tibetan teachers, living and dead, and from many of my colleagues and teachers. A few people who have been important include: Harvey Aronson, Anne Klein, Elizabeth Napper, Joe Wilson, Don Lopez, Dan Cozort, John Buescher, Kensur Yeshe Tupden, and Geshe Palden Dragpa (dGe bshes dPal ldan grags pa). I also thank Susan Kyser (at Snow Lion) and Nathan Lamphier for their comments on the ms. This book would never have existed without the efforts of Jeffrey Hopkins, Joshua Cutler (who conceived the project), Sidney Piburn (who pushed me to finish and publish the ms.), and H.H. the Dalai Lama.

Technical Note

In this book, Tibetan and Sanskrit terms are presented in English translation. Transliterations of key terms may be found in parentheses at the first appearance. Transliterations are based on the system described in Turrel Wylie's article, "A Standard System of Tibetan Transcription" (Harvard Journal of Asiatic Studies, 22, 1959, 261-276). Tibetan proper nouns appear in a rough phonetic form. These phonetic forms are not designed to indicate the exact pronunciation; they are intended only to give the reader a relatively easy-to-read approximate representation of the Tibetan name.

Chapter One
Two Truths in Four Systems

The two truths are (1) ultimate truths (*don dam bden pa, paramārtha-satya*) and (2) conventional truths (*kun rdzob bden pa, saṃvṛti-satya*). Explanations of the distinction between the two truths find a place in the assertions of each of the four tenet systems that are recognized by the Geluk order of Tibetan Buddhism as authentic formulations of Buddha's teaching. Just as the seal of a notary marks a document as authentic, these four systems each have four "seals," or views, that mark them as authentic Buddhist doctrine:

    1) all products are impermanent
    2) all contaminated things are miserable
    3) all phenomena are selfless
    4) nirvāṇa is peace

Ranked from the highest (that is, most profound) to the lowest, the four systems that share these views are:

    Great Vehicle (*mahāyāna*) tenet systems
        1) the Middle Way school (*mādhyamika*)
        2) the Mind Only school (*cittamātra*)

    Lesser Vehicle (*hīnayāna*) tenet systems
        3) the Sūtra school (*sautrāntika*)
        4) the Great Exposition school (*vaibhāṣika*)

There are subdivisions such as the Middle Way Autonomy and Middle Way Consequence branches of the Middle Way school, the Followers of Scripture and the Followers of Reasoning within the Sūtra school, etc. Still, Gelukpas traditionally claim that all who hold Buddhist tenets can be included within one of these four schools.[4] This does not comprise all Buddhists because there are many persons who have taken refuge in the three jewels from the depths of their hearts (and thus are Buddhists), but who do not propound Buddhist tenets. It is also said that to qualify as a proponent of a particular system, it is necessary actually to realize the selflessness taught by that system. Thus, for example, one does not become a proponent of the tenets of the Middle Way school until one first realizes emptiness as it is explained in the Middle Way school. The word translated as "tenet" (*grub mtha'*, *siddhānta*) means an "established conclusion," and thus a proponent of tenets is a not a person who is merely sympathetic with a certain position; it is a person who knows it to be correct and intends not to give it up.

However, what one system regards as a profound and definitive knowledge may be superficial or even wrong from the viewpoint of a "higher" system. The primary metaphor behind the Geluk study of tenets is not the time-line of Western scholarship, but a ladder on which the rungs are tenet systems. Each higher rung provides a better view than that below it, but only when one reaches the highest rung—the Middle Way Consequence school—does one see how things really exist. On the other hand, any rung on the ladder of Buddhist tenets gives a better view than one could get in the world, standing on the ground. The lower tenet systems, like rungs on a ladder, also provide a good means of access to the higher tenet-rungs.

Pushing the metaphor farther: Higher tenet-rungs may be dangerous for those not prepared for them. For some, it may be best to stay, for the time being, with a lower tenet system. On the other hand, it is not necessary that everyone move up the ladder of tenets one rung at a time. When one studies tenet systems, one moves through the systems one at a time, reflecting upon what one learns at each stage. However, when it comes to adopting the view of a tenet-system as one's own and seeking to develop realization of that view, the traditional advice is that one should find the highest view within the context of which one can maintain confidence in karmic cause and effect. One should not cultivate the view of the lowest system just because one feels humble.

We need to develop and to maintain confidence that our actions have consequences, that what we do makes a difference, that there are

persons who suffer, etc. In one sense, these teachings are more fundamental to Buddhism than teachings about emptiness. If one looks at
what most Buddhists in world actually do, one basically finds practices of giving, ethics, patience, and effort, motivated by a simple wish
to help others and/or to improve one's own prospects within cyclic
existence. Actual aspiration to escape cyclic existence and actual effort to realize emptiness are somewhat less common. Since they begin
with an innate tendency to reify rather than an innate tendency to
nihilism, the faith of ordinary Buddhists in persons, karma, ethics,
compassion, etc. is interwoven with this tendency to reify.

The yogi must try to eliminate factors of reification without destroying confidence in persons, karma, and so forth. If working with a
particular view is pushing one into the conviction that nothing mat-
ters, nothings exists, nothing makes a difference, it doesn't matter what
one does, etc., then one should back off and consider the views of a
"lower" tenet system. The higher rungs are dangerous because they
refute progressively more subtle types of reification. They therefore
increase the risk of slipping into nihilism.

The "views" that make one system higher than another include
various philosophical and psychological issues—the most important
of which is the question of what constitutes selflessness, or emptiness
(*stong pa nyid, śūnyatā*). The four tenet systems, therefore, should not
be confounded with the four sects, or orders (*chos lugs*), of Tibetan
Buddhism—Geluk, Sakya (Sa skya), Nyingma (rNying ma), and Kagyu
(bKa' brgyud)—which are commonly distinguished by the differences
in the types of ritual and meditation that they prefer. Kensur Yeshe
Tupden (Kensur Yeshey Thubden) explains that within each order there
are proponents of various tenet systems, as well as many other Buddhists who are not proponents of any tenet system.[5]

In the following pages, we will consider the two truths as they are
presented by each of these four tenet systems, beginning with the Great
Exposition system and proceeding through the Middle Way system.
We should note, however, that it is the highest system, the Middle
Way system, that gives greatest weight to the topic of the two truths.
The Great Exposition system and the Sūtra system devote much greater
attention to the four noble truths (true sufferings, true sources, true
cessations, and true paths), while the Mind Only system emphasizes
the "three natures" (thoroughly-established nature, other-powered
nature, and imputational nature). It is the Middle Way system that
discusses the two truths in the greatest depth and detail, and thus by

focusing on the two truths as they are seen by the four tenet systems we have to some degree imposed the program of the Middle Way system upon the three lower systems. We will approach the lower systems from an angle determined by the Middle Way system, thereby setting a backdrop against which we may better appreciate the presentation of the two truths in the Middle Way system.

Nāgārjuna, the philosophical pioneer of the Middle Way system, proclaimed the importance of the two truths in his *Treatise on the Middle Way*:

> The doctrines that Buddha taught are based upon two truths:
> Worldly conventional truths and truths that are ultimate objects.
> Those who do not know the distinction between these two truths
> Do not know the profound suchness in Buddha's teaching.[6]

In trying to understand the distinction between the two truths, it is well to begin by asking, What is it that the two truths are two types of? or, What is it that, when divided, gives us the two truths? Jamyang Shayba, who authored an important textbook on the Middle Way system, remarks that to talk about the distinction between the two truths without knowing their basis of division is like climbing out on the branches of a tree that has no roots.[7] Outside the Geluk tradition, there are many different assertions about the basis of division, but within the tradition there is agreement that the basis of division is objects of knowledge (*shes bya, jñeya*). The Gelukpa arguments for this position, which we will discuss later, are set forth specifically from the viewpoint of the Middle Way system—but the conclusion, that objects of knowledge are the basis of division of the two truths, can be carried over into the other three tenet systems.

It is critical to keep in mind that conventional truths and ultimate truths are not two types of viewpoint or perspective on the world, nor two "levels or reality," nor—as one might naturally expect—two types of truth. They are objects that exist and can be known. Existent (*yod pa*) and object of knowledge (*shes bya*) are equivalent—that is, whatever is one is the other. Since everything that exists is an object of knowledge, it follows that every existent must be one or the other of the two truths. The two truths are not confined to the realms of ideals and abstraction, as we might presume through familiarity with expressions such as, "beauty, truth, and goodness" and, "the truth will prevail." We can take anything that exists and ask, Is this a conventional truth or an ultimate truth? A table, for example, is a conventional truth according to the Middle Way system, the Mind Only system, and the Great Exposition system, but an ultimate truth according to the Sūtra System Following Reasoning.

By asserting that objects of knowledge are the basis of division of the two truths, Gelukpa teachers make the point that the two truths are knowable, accessible to understanding. Some systems teach that there are mysteries so deep or truths so profound that our minds—no matter how well-trained and purified—will never fathom them. According to the Geluk system, this is not the case. Indeed, some of the most important things, like emptiness, are extremely difficult to penetrate, and there are some things—such as the subtlest details of the relationship between a specific action and its moral effect—that only buddhas can know. However, even before one has become a bodhisattva, it is possible to realize the most profound emptiness, an ultimate truth, through the skillful use of reasoning within meditation. Moreover, each sentient being can and should aspire to transform his or her mind into the omniscient wisdom consciousness of a buddha, a mind that simultaneously and directly knows everything that exists—every ultimate truth and every conventional truth. Thus, the two truths are two types of things that we can know, and that we should aspire to know.

Chapter Two

The Great Exposition System

"Great Exposition system" is a broad designation for the eighteen sub-systems that emerged in the centuries following the Buddha's death. There are many different traditions regarding the number of schisms that occurred, the dates at which they occurred, and the names of the eighteen sects. The name "Great Exposition system" would seem to indicate that these systems mainly follow the *Great Detailed Exposition* (*māhavibhāṣa*), a compendium of teachings on the Seven Treatises of Manifest Knowledge (*abhidharma*). Only Great Exposition system sects hold that the Seven Treatises of Manifest Knowledge were spoken by the Buddha. In fact, however, not all of these systems rely upon the *Great Detailed Exposition*, and the name is a just a convenient designation around which to organize their assertions. The *Great Detailed Exposition* was not translated into Tibetan until the middle of the twentieth century, and has yet to make an impact on the Tibetan understanding of the Great Exposition system. Instead, Tibetan presentations of the tenets of the Great Exposition system rely on the *Treasury of Knowledge* written by Vasubandhu. Tibetan tradition holds that Vasubandhu was at first a follower of the Great Exposition system, was then a proponent of the Sūtra System Following Scripture, and was finally converted to the Mind Only system. The root text of his *Treasury of Knowledge* sets forth the tenets of the Great Exposition system while his commentary reflects the tenets of the Sūtra System Following Scripture.

Conventional Truths

Definitions of the two truths according to the Great Exposition system can be derived from this stanza in Vasubandhu's *Treasury of Knowledge*:

> If the awareness of something does not operate after that thing
> Is destroyed or mentally separated into other things,
> Then that thing exists conventionally, like a pot or water.
> Others exist ultimately.[8]

Accordingly, a conventional truth is defined as:

> a phenomenon which is such that if it were physically destroyed
> or mentally separated into parts, the consciousness apprehending
> it would be cancelled.

Note that this follows through on the idea that the two truths are divisions of objects of knowledge by defining a conventional truth in terms of how its destruction affects a consciousness. Although the two truths are objects (and not subjective perspectives), this definition points to the close relationship between minds and their objects. This theme becomes increasingly important in the higher tenet systems.

Vasubandhu gives a pot as an example of something that can be physically broken up into fragments, thereby eliminating the mind that sees a pot. A rosary is another example; when we look at a rosary, we have a consciousness apprehending a rosary. However, if we cut the rosary string, the consciousness apprehending a rosary will be cancelled, and a consciousness apprehending beads will be left in its place. We have all seen films of skyscrapers being demolished within seconds by strategically placed explosives. One minute there is a huge office building, seeming as real and solid as anything could be. A minute later there is a patch of sky over a pile of rock. When a building is demolished, the rubble is not a building; when a pot is broken, the shards are not a pot; when a rosary is undone, the beads are not a rosary. Thus, the consciousnesses apprehending a pot, a rosary, or a building are cancelled when those objects are destroyed.

Vasubandhu gives "water" as an example of something for which the consciousness apprehending it is cancelled, not by its physical destruction, but through its being mentally broken up into other phenomena. ("Water" here specifically refers to a general mass of water such as might be held in a pot; it does not refer to the "substance particle" water mentioned in the section on ultimate truths below.) Lacking techniques of modern science (e.g., electrolysis or blowing the water into superfine mist), the proponents of the Great Exposition system could see no way to physically cut a mass of water into something that no longer produces the apprehension of water. If we pour a portion of the water out of the pot, we still see water when we look into the pot. However, water can be broken down mentally, by separating out the qualities associated with water (such as its odor, taste, and touch)—qualities which are not themselves water. Water is apprehended in dependence upon these qualities coming together; when they are mentally disassembled, the consciousness apprehending water is cancelled.

Conventional truths are said to be of two types: (1) conventionalities that are shapes and (2) conventionalities that are collections. *Pot* is given as an example of the former, and *water* is given as an example of the latter. In fact, whatever is a conventional truth must also be a conventionality that is a collection. Some conventional truths, like a pot, are also shapes, while others, such as a mass of water, are not. When a conventional truth must have a certain shape in order to be perceived, then the mind apprehending it can be cancelled by physically destroying it. Thus, if we smash a pot with a hammer, we eliminate the shape in dependence upon which a pot is perceived. On the other hand, when a conventional truth does not depend upon the presence of a certain shape, the consciousness apprehending it cannot be cancelled by destroying it. In such cases, only the method of mentally pulling the object apart can be applied.

As to why such things as pots should be called "conventional truths" (*kun rdzob bden pa, saṃvṛti-satya*), let us first note that the word *kun rdzob* (*saṃvṛti*) has three distinct meanings: (1) obstructing the perception of reality, (2) interdependent, and (3) the conventional usage of the world.[9] By translating the term *kun rdzob bden pa* as "conventional truth," we are following the third meaning. However, the great Mongolian scholar Ngawang Palden (Ngag dband dpal ldan) argues that the second meaning of *kun rdzob*, "interdependent," is the most appropriate in the Great Exposition system.[10] A pot is an "interdependent truth" because when the various shapes of a pot—its bulbous sides, its flatness on the bottom, etc.—come into interdependence, then the statement, "A pot exists here," is true. Thus, in the Great Exposition system, the word "truth" (*bden pa, satya*) in the term "interdependent truth" simply refers to the existence of an object, or to the veracity of the statement that a certain object is present.

Conventional truth, conventionally existent (*kun rdzob tu yod, saṃvṛti-sat*), and imputedly existent (*btags yod, prajñapti-sat*) are equivalent in the Great Exposition system.

Ultimate Truths

The definition of an ultimate truth is:

> a phenomenon which is such that if it were physically destroyed
> or mentally separated into parts, the consciousness apprehending
> it would not be cancelled.

Examples include a directionally partless particle, a temporally partless moment of consciousness, and uncompounded space. In order to understand these examples, we must delve into the world of Buddhist particle theory.

According to proponents of the Great Exposition system, the gross objects of the material world are ultimately constituted of extremely subtle particles that lack any sort of spatial extension. Such particles are called directionally partless because they lack an east side and a west side, a top and a bottom, and so forth. However, these particles are only directionally partless, and not utterly partless, because each is a conglomeration of several "substance particles." Obviously, one cannot say that substance particles are smaller than conglomerate particles, because neither has even the slightest spatial extension. However, conglomerate particles can exist in isolation, while substance particles always exist together with other substance particles of different types as parts of a conglomerate particle. Within our realm, the Desire Realm, each conglomerate particle includes at least eight substance particles: earth, water, fire, air, form, smell, taste, and touch. If a conglomerate particle is part of the body of a sentient being, then it will have a ninth substance, the body sense faculty. If it is part of the sensing material of the eye, ear, nose, or tongue of a sentient being, then it will have a tenth substance corresponding to that sense faculty. If there is sound present, then there will be an eleventh substance particle, sound. In the Form Realm, the substance particles of odor and taste are absent, and thus conglomerate particles may have as few as six substance particles.

The proponents of the Great Exposition system have been challenged to explain how particles lacking spatial extension can come together to form objects that possess spatial extension. They respond by claiming that while each individual substance particle lacks the quality of "resistance" or "impenetrability" that keeps two things from being in the same place, directionally partless conglomerate particles do have such "resistance." Thus, since two conglomerate particles will not collapse into one another and occupy the same location, they can come together to build up gross material objects that have spatial extension. We may wonder how eight "resistanceless" substance particles can combine to form a "resistant" conglomerate.

Another question is: Do directionally partless conglomerate particles touch one another when they come together as the building blocks of an object that takes up space? Some proponents of the Great Exposition system say that they do. However, it seems impossible to explain how two particles without left and right sides could touch each other without effectively being in the same place, and thus failing to create extension. The Kashmiri subsystem of the Great Exposition system holds that directionally partless particles do not touch one another; they are held together by space.

In an analogous manner, proponents of the Great Exposition system maintain that a continuum of consciousness is built up from temporally partless or "durationless" instants of consciousness.

Since they have no parts, either spatially or temporally, partless particles and the subtlest instants of consciousness cannot be broken down or pulled apart so as to cause the mind apprehending them to be cancelled; thus they are classified as ultimate truths. It appears that most scholars hold that in the Great Exposition system both the directionally partless conglomerate particles and the substance particles are ultimate truths. (Again, this raises several questions that are open areas for inquiry. Can we not mentally separate the distinct substances of a directionally partless conglomerate? Why does this fail to cancel the mind apprehending the conglomerate?)

Another example of an ultimate truth is uncompounded space. This is not the space that is left over when one moves something, or digs a hole, nor is it the space of "outer space." In these senses, the word "space" refers to something that is impermanent and contingent upon the placement of objects. Uncompounded space extends in all directions as the context within which physical objects may or may not be present. It is the unchanging pervader of the material world, and is defined as the mere absence of obstructive contact. Ngawang Palden indicates that for proponents of the Great Exposition system and the Sūtra system, uncompounded space is partless.[11] There is certainly no way to destroy it physically. Even if we draw imaginary lines cutting it into various sections, none of these sections will be anything other than uncompounded space, and thus the consciousness apprehending it would not be cancelled.

Vasubandhu gives form (*gzugs, rupa*) as an example of an ultimate truth. His own commentary on his *Treasury of Knowledge* says, "Even if it is broken up into extremely subtle particles, or mentally separated into phenomena such as its taste, the awareness of the nature of form still operates."[12] If one physically destroys a form, the resulting parts are themselves form, and so the consciousness apprehending form is not cancelled. Even if one mentally isolates the component qualities of a form—i.e., its taste, odor, touch, and so forth—the consciousness apprehending form remains because each of these components is a form.

As mentioned above, the two truths do not rate as a topic of prime importance in the Great Exposition system writings and thus, for most phenomena, we can find no clear statement as to which of the two truths they are. What we have are simply the basic principles. Based on my understanding, I want to offer a few statements about how these principles might apply to particular examples.[13] First, each of the five aggregates (forms, feelings, discriminations, compositional factors, and consciousnesses) is an ultimate truth. Second, any collection of aggregates or continuum of moments of aggregates is an interdependent truth because when it is mentally separated into its parts, it is no longer apprehended as a collection or continuum. Finally, although a partless "substance particle" is an ultimate truth, a directionally partless conglomerate particle should be considered an interdependent truth because it can be mentally disassembled into a set of diverse constituent substance particles.

According to Ngawang Palden, the word "ultimate" (*don dam, paramārtha*) in the term "ultimate truth" (*don dam bden pa, paramārtha-satya*) refers to something that does not depend on parts, and the word "truth" (*bden pa, satya*) means something that can be known, through reasoning or otherwise.[14] He raises the point that even a substance particle is interdependent in one sense because it is always coexistent with at least five other substance particles. However, it is still an ultimate truth because the mind apprehending it does not depend upon these other substances. The other substance particles are not its parts and it is not imputed to the collection of other substance particles with which it coexists. Rather, it exists in a substantial manner. To be substantially existent (*rdzas su yod, dravya-sat*) is equivalent to being an ultimate truth, and also equivalent to being ultimately established (*don dam du grub pa, paramārtha-siddha*).

Selflessness

In general, the two Great Vehicle tenet systems (the Mind Only system and the Middle Way system) are said to be distinguished from the two Lesser Vehicle tenet systems (the Great Exposition system and the Sūtra system) in that the two higher systems teach the emptiness, or selflessness, of all phenomena, while the lower systems teach only a selflessness of persons. Although the lower systems do admit the existence of a bodhisattva path (leading to buddhahood) for a few rare individuals, they are mainly concerned with the attainment of liberation from cyclic existence in the less fully enlightened condition of an *arhat*. Sentient beings are trapped in cyclic existence by certain mistaken conceptions about the type of "self" that a person has. Toward this end, proponents of the Great Exposition system recommend meditation on the non-existence of a permanent, partless, and independent self of persons. Thirteen of the eighteen Great Exposition subsystems hold that this is only a coarse selflessness and that the subtle selflessness that must be realized is the non-existence of a substantially existent or self-sufficient self of persons.

The Great Vehicle tenet systems teach a selflessness of phenomena because it is only by realizing the real nature of all phenomena that one can come, at the end of the path, to omniscience in the state of buddhahood. Omniscience here refers to a consciousness directly and simultaneously realizing all ultimate truths and all conventional truths. Bodhisattvas seek omniscience in order to perfect and maximize their capacity to help others. Proponents of the Great Exposition system do not teach this sort of omniscience, and perhaps it can be argued on these grounds that they do not have a full presentation of a selflessness of phenomena according to the Great Vehicle type. However, as Geshe Palden Dragpa has argued, there does seem to be a "selflessness of phenomena" presentation implicit in these investigations of how a pot or a mass of water, for example, is imputedly existent insofar as it is apprehended only in dependence upon the aggregation of certain shapes and parts.[15]

This presentation of the two truths brings home the message that we have an ingrained predilection to see a gross sort of wholeness in our selves, our bodies, and the external objects we encounter. We fail to reflect upon the fact that such phenomena are imputed to collections of parts. Consequently, in our minds they take on a solidity and substantiality which they actually do not have. The conventional truths of the Great Exposition system are subject to disintegration, but we ignorantly apprehend them as unchanging and permanent. We mistakenly see them as independent realities, when in fact they rely on the aggregation of things other than themselves. All of these misapprehensions lead us into afflictive emotions, such as desire and hatred, and these afflictions in turn motivate the actions that trap us in a cycle of suffering.

Yogis can notice and experience the very subtlest substance particles and partless instants of consciousness. According to the Great Exposition system, they thereby eradicate the ignorant conceptions of a permanent, partless, and independent self and/or a substantially existent self, and eventually attain nirvāṇa, which is a true cessation. The *Great Detailed Explanation* includes a multiplicity of conflicting opinions about how the two truths are related to the four noble truths, but the Geluk presentation of the Great Exposition system decisively classifies nirvāṇa as an ultimate truth. This is not because nirvāṇa is the ultimate object of attainment at the end of the path, but simply because it meets the definition of ultimate truth given above. While the distinction between ultimate truths and conventional truths implies a preference for the former, none of the four tenets systems holds that "ultimate truth" refers to the ultimate goal of the path.

Chapter Three
The Sūtra System

The Geluk presentation of the two truths as seen by the Sūtra system may seem strange at first, especially in its assertions that ordinary objects such as tables and chairs are ultimate truths, while the emptiness, or selflessness, that must be realized on the path is a conventional truth. Many non-Gelukpas, both in Tibet and in the West, have given radically different interpretations of the Sūtra system.[16] However, the Geluk approach to this system introduces several critical concepts—such as the relationship between direct perception and conceptual thought—that are in large measure carried over into the Geluk presentation of the Middle Way system. In fact, the tenets of the Sūtra system are the bedrock of the curriculum in Geluk monastic colleges. Before taking up the study of higher systems, monks traditionally dedicate many years to the study of the logic, psychology, and epistemology of the Sūtra system. Therefore, anyone who wants to understand how Gelukpas approach the Middle Way system must understand the Geluk presentation of the Sūtra system.

All Buddhist tenet systems rely on Buddhist sūtras. However, as indicated by its name, the Sūtra system emphasizes that its tenets derive mainly from the texts that it classifies as sūtras. Unlike the Great Exposition system, the Sūtra system does not regard the Seven Treatises of Knowledge (*chos mngon pa, abhidharma*) as having been spoken by Buddha. Also, from the viewpoint of the Sūtra system, the Great Vehicle (*mahāyāna*) sūtras are not really the word of Buddha.[17]

There are two main subsystems of the Sūtra system: the Followers of Scripture and the Followers of Reasoning. The viewpoint of the Followers of Scripture is epitomized in Vasubandhu's *Explanation of the "Treasury of Knowledge."* The presentation of the two truths found therein fully accords with the explanation of the two truths in the Great Exposition system. Since that system was explained above, this section will deal exclusively with the two truths as presented by the proponents of the Sūtra system who are Followers of Reasoning. Hereafter, for the sake of simplicity, the system of the proponents of the Sūtra system who are Followers of Reasoning will be referred to as the "Sūtra system." The most important original source for this system is Dharmakīrti's *Commentary on (Dignāga's) "Compendium on Valid Cognition."*

Equivalents and Examples

Anything that exists must be either an ultimate truth or a conventional truth, and there is nothing that is both. Some initial sense of the two truths in the Sūtra system may be gained by considering the other phenomena with which they are equivalent.[18] The following terms state equivalents of "ultimate truth":

1) functioning thing (*dngos po*)
2) impermanent phenomenon (*mi rtag pa*)
3) specifically characterized phenomenon (*rang mtshan*)
4) appearing object of direct perception (*mngon sum gyi snang yul*)
5) that which is truly established (*bden grub*)
6) that which ultimately exists (*don dam par yod*)

Ultimate truth is coextensive with each of its equivalents. This means, for example, that whatever is a functioning thing is necessarily an ultimate truth and whatever is an ultimate truth is necessarily a functioning thing.

In the term "impermanent phenomenon," "impermanent" does not simply mean that something will eventually end; it means that something changes and disintegrates instant by instant. Examples of ultimate truths are: tables, chairs, houses, persons, pots, small particles, etc.

The following terms state the coextensive equivalents of "conventional truth":

1) non-functioning phenomenon (*dngos med*)
2) permanent phenomenon (*rtag pa*)
3) generally characterized phenomenon (*spyi mtshan*)
4) appearing object of a conceptual consciousness (*rtog pa'i*

snang yul)
5) that which is falsely established (*brdzun par grub pa*)
6) that which exists conventionally (*kun rdzob tu yod*)

Examples of conventional truths include: a generic meaning-image of a table, the uncompounded space that is the mere absence of obstructive contact, and a person's emptiness of being substantially existent.

Conceptual Consciousness

According to the Geluk interpretation of the Followers of Reasoning of the Sūtra system, the distinction between the two truths is closely bound up with the distinction between conceptual consciousnesses (*rtog pa, kalpanā*) and direct perceivers (*mngon sum, pratyakṣa*). To be exact, the appearing objects of conceptual consciousnesses are always conventional truths and the appearing objects of direct perceivers are always ultimate truths. Thus, in order to understand the two truths in this system, one must understand the distinction between conceptuality and direct perception.

For each consciousness, we can distinguish two types of objects: (1) its appearing object (*snang yul*) and (2) its object of engagement (*'jug yul*). For a conceptual consciousness, the appearing object and the object of engagement are quite different. For example, in the case of a conceptual consciousness apprehending a table, the object of engagement, what is being understood or "gotten at," is simply the table. However, the appearing object of that mind is not the table itself but an image conveying the generic meaning of "table," an image that is isolated from the richness of detail that appears to direct perception. A conceptual consciousness apprehending a table has an appearance of "table" that is isolated from the particular qualities that are always right with a table—such as a table's color, shape, impermanence, existence, and so forth.

Conceptual consciousnesses are of many different types. Memory consciousness, consciousnesses of imagination and visualization, doubting consciousnesses, intellectual speculations, conceptual understandings derived from meditative reasoning, profoundly ignorant misconceptions that trap sentient beings in cyclic existence, and ordinary consciousnesses thinking of tables, chairs, or ice cream: all of these are conceptual consciousnesses. Although wildly disparate in many ways, these consciousnesses are alike in being unable to perceive all the specific characteristics or qualities (color, shape, impermanence, etc.) of their objects of engagement.

Conceptual consciousnesses are called "eliminative engagers" (*sel 'jug*) because they get at their objects in an indirect way, by eliminating everything other than just that very object. When everything other than "table" is eliminated, this obviously strips away chairs, clocks, and so forth. It also strips away a table's color, impermanence, and so forth, as well as all specific instances of table, because these qualities and particular instances are not themselves identical to "table." However, when a table has been conceptually stripped of all its specific characteristics and formulated in isolation as a mental image, what remains is not an actual table. What remains is a mental "construction" of the opposite-of-not-being-one-with-table. This is the relatively abstract generic image of "table" that appears to a conceptual consciousness apprehending a table. It is a generally characterized phenomenon because it, unlike a table, is not made from wood, etc. and hence is not established by way of its own character. It lacks the specific details and qualities of any particular table.

While this process sounds incredibly cumbersome, it occurs effortlessly—almost automatically—when we think of an already familiar object. The work of learning something new, something we do not already understand—like emptiness—is the work of creating and gradually refining a new generic image.

When the mind remembers or thinks about an ice cream cone, for example, the ice cream cone is the object of engagement and a generic meaning-image of an ice cream cone is the appearing object. To this conceptual consciousness, the generic meaning-image of the ice cream appears as though it were an ice cream cone. Normally, of course, we would never become so confused as to actually *think*, "This image of the ice cream cone that is appearing to me is an actual ice cream cone." On the other hand, conceptual thought uses these abstract images, manipulating them *as though they were the actual objects* that they represent. In other words, all conceptual thought (whether accurate or not) has a factor of mistakenness because symbolic images of objects appear to it as though they were the actual objects.

This kind of deceptive appearance is compared to the way that a mirror image of face appears to be a face. We get valuable information about the condition of our own faces by allowing our senses to be fooled, superficially, in this way. Analogously, it is critical to the Geluk presentation of the path that conceptual consciousnesses, despite having mistaken appearance, can be authoritative knowers of their objects of engagement. What is more, unlike direct perceivers—which in the Sūtra system can realize only impermanent phenomena—conceptual consciousness can realize *all* types of phenomena.

Generic meaning-images are permanent, i.e., they are not subject to moment-by-moment change and disintegration. They last only as long as the mind to which they appear, but during that time they do not change from one moment to the next.[19] All permanent phenomena (e.g., generic meaning-images, uncompounded space, etc.) are conventional truths. Here, the term translated as "conventional truth" (*kun rdzob bden pa, saṃvṛti-satya*) really means "truth for an obscured awareness," and in this context "obscured awareness" includes all conceptual consciousnesses. A conceptual consciousness is called an "obscured awareness" because it is obscured with regard to the specific characteristics of impermanent phenomena. It is obscured with regard to these characteristics in the sense that it cannot collectively experience their variegated complexity. For example, when a conceptual consciousness takes a particular table as its object of engagement, it is by nature unable to experience holistically the specific and unique characteristics of that table. Instead, its appearing object is a meaning-image that represents an abstraction of a table.

Such an abstraction comes to mind when a person who understands English hears the word "table." The conceptual consciousnesses of beings who know a language frequently associate a meaning-image with the sound-image of the corresponding word. However, conceptual thought does not require linguistic capacity. Animals, for example, must have generic meaning-images representing things like "food" and "danger"—even though they have no words to associate with these meanings. Also, even sentient beings who know a language have some conceptual consciousnesses that are without any linguistic component. Einstein, for example, said that he could think without language. (Is this what we call "intuition"?)

Direct Perception

Now, let us consider the workings of the non-conceptual consciousnesses known as direct perceivers. Impermanent phenomena (those that disintegrate moment by moment) are called ultimate truths because they are truths for the ultimate consciousnesses. This means that they exist for, or fully appear to, direct perception. Here, "ultimate consciousnesses" include all direct perceivers—not only the direct realizations of yogis, but also the ordinary, correct sense consciousnesses perceiving tables, etc.

In the case of an eye consciousness directly perceiving a table, the table is both the appearing object and the object of engagement. There is no appearing object apart from the particular table that the eye consciousness apprehends. This means that a particular table is known in direct perception through the vivid appearance of that particular table. A table appears by casting its aspect to the consciousness, which then takes on that aspect. In a sense, the eye consciousness directly perceiving a table is like a mirror that bears the exact likeness of that particular table, including all of its specific characteristics—such as the table's color, shape, size, impermanence, etc. Only a specifically characterized phenomenon (that is, an ultimate truth, i.e., an impermanent phenomenon) is able cast an aspect to a consciousness, and thus only ultimate truths can be explicitly realized in direct perception.

An ultimate truth, such as a table, fully appears to the ordinary eye consciousness directly apprehending it because it appears together with all of its specific characteristics or qualities, such as its color, size, etc. A direct perceiver is called a "collective engager" or "holistic engager" (*sgrub 'jug*) because it gets at its object via the collective appearance of every particular that is one substantial entity, or "part and parcel," with its object. A table appears to an eye consciousness in all its individuality. Every one of that particular table's unique qualities appears to that eye consciousness. Even the table's quality of disintegrating moment by moment appears to that eye consciousness.

However, it is very important to remember that direct perceivers do not necessarily ascertain or notice or realize all of these details. Even though a table's subtle impermanence (i.e., its quality of disintegrating moment by moment) appears, it is not noticed, or ascertained, by an ordinary eye consciousness apprehending a table. The mere appearance of impermanence does not help on the path unless it is realized. In order to realize subtle impermanence with direct perception, it is necessary first to realize it with a conceptual, inferential consciousness. Thus, the Geluk presentation of the Sūtra system anticipates an absolutely vital point in the Geluk presentation of the Middle Way system: Despite the mistakenness of conceptuality, valid conceptual understandings reached through careful reasoning are indispensable stepping-stones to yogic direct perception.

By reading and reviewing the foregoing discussion of conceptual consciousnesses and direct perceivers, one can get an idea of how (1) permanent phenomenon, (2) conventional truth, (3) appearing object of a conceptual consciousness, and (4) generally characterized phenomenon are equivalent, while (1) impermanent phenomenon, (2) ultimate truth, (3) appearing object of direct perception and (4) specifically characterized phenomenon are equivalent. Now let us see how Gelukpas actually define the two truths in the Sūtra system.

Definitions

Dharmakirti's *Commentary on (Dignāga's) "Compendium on Valid Cognition"* says:

> That which is ultimately able to perform a function exists ultimately here [in this system]; other [phenomena, which are not ultimately able to perform a function] exist conventionally. These describe specifically and generally characterized phenomena.[20]

Some Gelukpa scholars use this passage as a source for definitions of specifically characterized and generally characterized phenomena rather than as a source for definitions of ultimate truth and conventional truth. However, others (such as Purbujok [Phur bu lcog] and Jamyang Chokla Öser ['Jam dbyang phyogs lha 'od zer]) define an ultimate truth as:

> that which is ultimately able to perform a function.

Conventional truths are defined as phenomena that are not ultimately able to perform functions.

What does it mean to perform a function? Ultimate truths (impermanent phenomena) are able to function as causes, that is, they are able to carry out the function of producing effects. As they disintegrate moment by moment, ultimate truths are able to act as causes for phenomena in the next moment. For example, one moment of a flame may produce the next moment of flame in that continuum; the last moment of a flame produces the effect of smoke.

In addition, there is a second important type of function that any ultimate truth can perform, and which no conventional truth can perform: to serve as a cause for the production of an eye consciousness directly perceiving it. In contrast, a conventional truth—which is a permanent, static phenomenon—cannot carry out a function or produce an effect. It does not change moment by moment, and it is unable to produce a consciousness apprehending it.

Mental images and other conventional truths do not exist as actual things that can function. They cannot be causes of consciousnesses because they are, in fact, the mere "constructions," or mere imputations, of a conceptual mind. This understanding is the basis for another Geluk approach to defining the two truths in this system. Ngawang Palden (Ngag dbang dPal ldan), for example, defines a conventional truth as:

> a phenomenon which is established as a mere imputation by a conceptual consciousness

and defines an ultimate truth as:

> a phenomenon that exists from its own side, without being merely imputed by a conceptual consciousness.[21]

An impermanent phenomenon, such as a table, meets this definition of an ultimate truth because it has its own type of existence, apart from conceptual imputation. A table is an ultimate truth, something that ultimately exists, because it is produced from causes and conditions, is not just imputed by thought, and can cast the aspect of its own specific, unique characteristics to a perceiving consciousness. In contrast, permanent phenomena, such as meaning-images and uncompounded space, are conventional truths because they are not produced from causes and conditions, are only imputed by conceptuality, and have no specific characteristics that can appear to a direct perceiver. They are only conventionally existent or imputedly existent (*btags yod*).

However, it should be noted that even things that are only imputedly existent do exist. To exist as a mere conceptual imputation does not mean to be a non-existent that is only imagined to exist. Take the example of the horns of a rabbit. They do not exist as a mere imputation by a conceptual consciousness because they do not exist at all. On the other hand, in the consciousness of someone imagining the horns of a rabbit, there is a meaning-image of the horns of a rabbit. This meaning-image exists; it exists as a mere imputation by a conceptual consciousness. In the Geluk presentation of the Sūtra system, things that are only imputedly existent do exist. Later, we will see that in the highest system, the Middle Way Consequence system, all phenomena are regarded as mere imputations by conceptuality—even those that are able to work as causes.

Selflessness of Persons

According to the Sūtra system, escape from cyclic existence depends upon the realization that the person is empty of being substantially existent in the sense of being self-sufficient. Persons are impermanent phenomena, and therefore they are ultimate truths. They are capable of producing effects, and they can cast their uncommon aspects to a direct perceiver. However, unlike many other ultimate truths, persons are not self-sufficient because they cannot be known without the cognition of some part of the mind or body to which they are imputed. Roughly speaking, a person lacks both the material "substance" of the body and the psychic "substance" of consciousness. The person is imputed to certain aggregates of mind and/or matter, and thus all its functions, including the activity of casting an aspect to a direct perceiver apprehending it, are dependent upon the functioning of those aggregates.

The ignorant consciousness that is the root of suffering in cyclic existence is a consciousness conceiving the person to exist in a substantial, self-sufficient manner. According to the Sūtra system, it is only the person that is innately misapprehended in this way. Therefore, the goal of the yogi following this system is to generate a wisdom consciousness realizing the emptiness that is the mere absence of a substantially existent, self-sufficient person.

However, it is impossible for a sentient being to have a direct perceiver that explicitly realizes such an emptiness because emptiness is an uncompounded, permanent phenomenon. Emptiness is thus a conventional truth; it is a generally characterized phenomenon. An emptiness lacks specific, uncommon characteristics that can appear to a direct perceiver, and thus cannot be known directly. Therefore, the Sūtra system maintains that the ultimate wisdom consciousness is a direct perceiver that directly and explicitly cognizes the mental and physical aggregates in such a manner that it thereby implicitly realizes the absence of a self-sufficient person in relation to those aggregates.

Conclusion

In a great many ways, the study of the Geluk presentation of the Sūtra system prepares the mind for study of the Middle Way system. Several of these ways pertain to topics not covered here—such as positive (*sgrub pa, vidhi*) and negative phenomena (*dgag pa, pratiṣedha*), generality (*spyi, sāmānya*) and particularity (*bye brag, viśeṣa*), and the use of logical signs (*rtags, liṅga*) in meditative reasoning. Still, several of the most important points can be drawn from the material just explained.

First, the Sūtra system introduces the idea that the two truths are objects of two distinct types of awareness, conceptual consciousnesses and direct perceivers. Although conceptual consciousnesses are not always valid knowers (*tshad ma, pramāṇa*), in general both conceptual consciousnesses and direct perceivers are capable of validly knowing their objects. The idea that the two truths are two circles of objects, each appearing to a particular type of mind and not discredited by the other, is extremely important in the Geluk presentation of the Middle Way system and is a key to understanding why Gelukpas insist that the two truths are logically compatible rather than a transcendental paradox. Each of the two truths is a certain type of object for a certain type of mind, and neither knocks the other out. In the Middle Way system, the two truths are objects found by conventional and ultimate valid cognizers, whereas in the Sūtra system they are the appearing objects of conceptual consciousnesses and direct perceivers. The parallel between the two presentations is rough, but worth noting. The Gelukpa presentation of the Sūtra system probably instills students with a basic trust in the compatibility of the two truths, a trust which provides a foundation for the study of the two truths in the Middle Way system.

Second, the Sūtra system is the context in which Gelukpas introduce students to the idea that conceptuality, far from being the enemy, is an absolutely indispensable tool on the path to liberation. For example, the Sūtra system holds that the subtle impermanence of a table already appears to an ordinary eye consciousness directly perceiving the table; however, this impermanence remains unnoticed, and we therefore mistakenly conceive of the table as something that stays the same from one moment to the next. In order to realize in direct perception the subtle impermanence of the table, it is first necessary to form a conceptual understanding that the table does change moment by moment. Beginning with a doubt (*the tshom*) or a suspicion that the table may actually change moment by moment, meditation on the impermanence of the table gradually leads to a very strong sense, a correct assumption (*yid dpyod*), that the table is impermanent. Still further meditation leads to a fully valid inferential certainty (*rjes dpag tshad ma*) that the table is impermanent. From first suspicion to final certainty, all of these consciousnesses are conceptual. Through repeatedly meditating on subtle impermanence in this way, one gains an ever deeper familiarity with it—until ultimately one may realize it in direct perception. Thus, conceptuality is first wielded as a sword against a misconception, and dropped only when that misconception has been refuted. This pattern is echoed in Geluk descriptions of how emptiness is realized in the Middle Way system. Tsong Khapa (Tsong kha pa) stresses that it is not enough to withdraw into a non-conceptual trance where the conception of inherent existence (along with all other conceptual consciousnesses) has been suppressed temporarily. One must begin by using conceptual meditations to identify and logically refute the conception of inherent existence.

Third, the Sūtra system equalizes the status of parts and wholes—in contrast to the Great Exposition system. As we have seen above, the Great Exposition system holds that things are ultimately real if they are irreducible to parts that are other than themselves. Roughly speaking, this means that irreducible parts are really real, while the "wholes" or composites that are built from these parts are only conventionally real. In contrast, the Geluk interpretation of the Sūtra system holds that even gross collections of particles—chairs, table, etc.—exist in an ultimate sense because they are appearing objects of direct perception. Anne Klein has pointed out that one of the unique features of the Geluk version of the Sūtra system is that (unlike the Great Exposition system and unlike non-Geluk presentations of the Sūtra system) it prepares the mind to accept the equalization of the reality-status of parts and wholes that is taught in the Middle Way system.[22] In the Middle Way system, there are no partless particles, no irreducible elements. Parts are neither more nor less real than wholes because all phenomena exist in a merely conventional manner.

Furthermore, the Sūtra system helps to prepare the mind for study of the Middle Way Consequence system by introducing the idea that something can exist even though it is merely imputed by conceptuality. For example, having become familiar with the idea that the extremely valuable selflessness of a person is a "mere imputation by conceptuality," the student will not make the mistake of assuming that the phrase "mere imputation by conceptuality" refers to what only seems to exist but in fact does not exist at all. This is a valuable inoculation against the danger of nihilism when later studying the Middle Way system's doctrine that all phenomena exist as mere imputations by conceptuality.

Finally, the Sūtra system insists that things can work (i.e., carry out functions, act as causes) only if they exist in an ultimate sense, from their own side, and not just as imputations by conceptuality. This assertion, which is utterly contrary to the view of the Middle Way Consequence system, is like a target that Gelukpa teachers set up in the minds of their students. It draws an aspect of our innate, worldly way of thinking out of the shadows and into the focus of awareness. Later, when the study of the Middle Way system is taken up, the arguments of that higher system will already have a clear target at which to aim and strike.

Chapter Four

Great Vehicle Tenet Systems

Atiśa's enormously influential *Lamp for the Path* divides persons into three groups according to their capacity.[23] Persons of small capacity think mainly about their temporary welfare, comfort, and pleasure within cyclic existence. They are deeply attached to cyclic existence and do not wish to leave it. Some persons of small capacity mainly seek pleasure in this lifetime through non-religious or nominally religious techniques; others, the lowest of actual religious practitioners, rely on religious practices mainly for the sake of a good rebirth in a future lifetime. Those of small capacity have not yet achieved a path that can bestow liberation. In contrast, persons of intermediate capacity mainly seek their own liberation from cyclic existence. They have turned away from cyclic existence and set their hearts on nirvāṇa. However, the path that they follow is a Lesser Vehicle (*hīnayāna*) path because, concerned mainly about their own welfare, they do not take up the burden of saving all beings. Persons of great capacity, on the other hand, altruistically undertake to bring happiness to all sentient beings. When they realize the possibility of becoming buddhas themselves, and understand that the powers of a buddha will enable them to give others the best possible help, they resolve to practice as long as is necessary in order to attain buddhahood for the sake of all sentient beings. This resolve is the aspiration of a bodhisattva, and those who have this aspiration have set out upon a Great Vehicle (*mahāyāna*) path.

Thus, the Lesser Vehicle/Great Vehicle distinction refers to two different types of path. Lesser Vehicle paths are motivated by a wish to leave cyclic existence and culminate in a state of solitary, peaceful liberation. Great Vehicle paths are motivated by vast compassion for all sentient beings and culminate in the state of a perfect, omniscient, blissful buddha. However, as we noted at the very beginning of this essay, there is also a distinction between Lesser Vehicle tenet systems and Great Vehicle tenet systems. These two types of Lesser Vehicle/ Great Vehicle distinction should not be confused. Briefly, Lesser Vehicle and Great Vehicle paths are distinguished by their motivation, their aspiration. Lesser Vehicle and Great Vehicle tenet systems are not distinguished by motivation; they are distinguished by their view of selflessness, or emptiness.

Unlike the Lesser Vehicle tenet systems, which teach only a selflessness of persons, the Great Vehicle tenet systems teach that the most profound reality, the most subtle and important type of selflessness, is a selflessness, or emptiness, that is a quality of all phenomena. They hold that the bodhisattva trains in altruistically motivated meditation on the emptiness of all phenomena, thus preparing for the omniscience of buddhahood. Some Great Vehicle systems maintain that Lesser Vehicle practitioners do not realize the profound emptiness of phenomena at all and are therefore unable to overcome the obstructions to omniscience. However, the highest system, the Middle Way Consequence system, holds that persons on Lesser Vehicle paths do realize emptiness, but are unable to achieve omniscience on their paths because their wisdom is not empowered by association with altruism and altruistically motivated actions of giving, ethics, patience, etc.

The Two Truths as One Entity

The Great Vehicle tenet systems teach that the subtle and profound emptiness realized on the bodhisattva path is an ultimate truth. This ultimate truth is a negative phenomenon—the mere absence of a certain type of self (i.e., a certain kind of existence) in phenomena. The various Great Vehicle systems disagree about the kind of existence that emptiness negates. The Mind Only system, for example, says that emptiness is the absence of a difference of entity between an object and the mind apprehending it, while the Middle Way Consequence system says that emptiness is the absence of inherent existence. Still, however they define it, Great Vehicle tenet systems agree that the subtle emptiness is (1) an ultimate truth, and (2) a quality present in all phenomena. That is, everything that exists (including emptiness itself) is devoid of whatever type of existence emptiness negates.

Conventional truths include all phenomena other than emptiness— tables, chairs, etc. All of these phenomena are necessarily empty (*stong pa, śūnya*). They are not themselves emptinesses (*stong pa nyid, śūnyatā*), but they are empty because they lack a certain type of existence. Since conventional truths have the quality of being empty, and since emptiness is an ultimate truth, it follows that ultimate truths and conventional truths are distinct, mutually exclusive phenomena that exist inseparably, right together as a single entity. The *Sūtra Unravelling the Thought* compares the relationship between the two truths to the relationship between a white conch shell and its whiteness, pepper and its hot taste, cotton and its softness, and other similar pairs. In the relationship between a white shell and its whiteness, the whiteness is not the shell, and the shell is not the whiteness; still, the white shell is always white.[24] Similarly, Gelukpas argue, it is not a paradox that the two truths can be mutually exclusive within a single entity. Like whiteness and a white shell, they are quality and quality-possessor. Emptiness is the highest quality, the final nature, of every phenomenon.

Chapter Five

The Mind Only System

The Mind Only system derives its name from its assertion that there are no objects external to, i.e., of a different entity than, the consciousness perceiving them. This does not mean that only consciousnesses exist. It means that nothing exists divorced from, external to, or independent of consciousness. Rather than regarding mind as something that reflects and responds to a pre-existent outside world, the Mind Only system sees a mind and its object as phenomena that come into existence simultaneously, from a single karmic cause. Moment by moment the world arises, in its subjective and objective aspects, as the effect of latencies left with the mind by former actions.

The Mind Only system is defined in terms of its refutation of external objects and its assertion that impermanent, functional phenomena (such as consciousnesses, tables, chairs, etc.) truly exist (*bden par yod*). Among those who share these positions, there are two types: Followers of Scripture and Followers of Reasoning. Among proponents of the Mind Only system, those who are Followers of Scripture rely mainly on Asaṅga's *Five Treatises on the Levels*, which comment mainly on the *Sūtra Unravelling the Thought*. Geluk tradition holds that Asaṅga lived for 150 years during which, even though his own final system was the Middle Way Consequence system, he mainly advanced Mind Only views in order to convert his brother Vasubandhu to the Great Vehicle. The proponents of the Mind Only system who are Followers of Reasoning rely mainly on Dignāga and on Dharmakīrti's works on valid cognition. The term "proponent of Mind Only" frequently refers to the Followers of Scripture, and their views are our focus here.

Mind Creates the World

Buddhists do not assert the existence of a single, all-powerful, personal Lord of the Universe who created the world and the beings within it. In general, Buddhists believe that time is beginningless and that the various phenomena that we see and experience are effects, direct or indirect, of our own consciousnesses. The world we are born into is determined by our past actions (*las, karma*). Most Buddhists agree that an "action" or karma is really the intention (*sems pa, cetanā*) that accompanies an activity of body, speech, or mind. Since intention is a mental factor, a type of consciousness, it can be said that mind is the principal creator of all environments and beings. In the *Collection of Related Teachings*, the Buddha says:

> The world is led by mind
> And drawn by mind.
> All phenomena are controlled
> By one phenomenon, mind.[25]

And Candrakīrti's *Supplement to the Middle Way* says:

> Buddha teaches that the complex worlds of sentient beings
> And their environments are established only by mind;
> All transmigrating beings are born from actions.[26]

Thus, it is said that you can know what kind of mind you had in the past by looking at the world and the body you have today; you can know what kind of world and body you will have in the future by looking at the mind you have today.

While past minds control present objects through the "law of karma," there is another, even more immediate way in which our minds affect what we can experience. In every instant of the ongoing process of cognition we are blocked or screened off from knowing things as they really are because our minds operate under the influence of ignorance (*ma rig pa, avidyā*). Ignorance is not the condition of not knowing, but an actual consciousness that wrongly conceives the way things exist. The most important type of ignorance, an ignorance that we possess innately, is a mind that misconceives phenomena to exist in a manner directly contrary to their actual mode of existence. While phenomena are actually empty and selfless, ignorance erroneously apprehends the non-empty and self. Even when it is not manifestly present, ignorance implicitly conditions the way we see the world. This unwarranted over-reification, or exaggeration, of the way things exist is extremely pernicious because it allows other afflictive emotions—desire, hatred, jealousy, anger, and so forth—to bite into our minds. Afflictive emotions contaminate the action (i.e., the intention) with which they are associated, leading to future rebirth. Thus ignorance, an erroneous consciousness, is the root of suffering in cyclic existence.

Study of the tenets of the Mind Only system promotes understanding of the key Buddhist teaching that mind is the source of all suffering and all happiness, the source of cyclic existence and nirvāṇa. Although proponents of most other tenet systems do not agree with the Mind Only assertion that there are no external objects, they may still value and appreciate the Mind Only system for the special attention it gives to the power and primacy of mind. Thus, the great Geluk scholar Gung Tang (Gung thang) writes:

> It is appropriate for the discerning individual, who knows that the basis for all happiness and suffering is only his own mind, to rely on this system.[27]

Mind Only

How does an action completed years or lifetimes or eons ago control what we experience today? For the law of karma to work, actions must leave behind some trace, and that trace must somehow be able to continue from the time of the action until the time of its effect. The Mind Only system of Asaṅga and his followers posits a special consciousness called the "mind-basis-of-all" (*kun gzhi rnam shes, ālaya-vijñāna*) that serves as the basis into which actions infuse their latencies. While other Buddhist systems posit six types of consciousness (the five sense consciousnesses and the mental consciousness), the Mind Only system adds a seventh mind called afflicted mentality (which we will describe below) and an eighth, the mind-basis-of-all.

A complete action of body, speech, or mind leaves a latency with the mind-basis-of-all. These latencies are neither mind nor form, but are assigned to the category "compositional factor" (*'du byed, saṃskāra*). They are called predispositions (*bag chags, vāsanā*) or seeds (*sa bon, bīja*) because they have the potential to ripen into new experiences. Seeds remain with the mind-basis-of-all until necessary cooperating causes come together and karmic fruition occurs. The cooperating causes that bring certain seeds to fruition are other consciousnesses in the continuum of that person—perhaps a certain series of mental consciousnesses—that influence the ripening of seeds in the mind-basis-of-all.

Most Buddhist systems other than the Mind Only system hold that the objects that we experience are among the causes of the consciousness apprehending them. Suppose, for example, that in moment #1 there are three things present: (1) the sense faculty of an eye, (2) a consciousness, and (3) a blue table. These three act as causes for the arising, in moment #2, of an eye consciousness apprehending a blue table. Since a table is an impermanent phenomenon, changing and disintegrating moment by moment, the blue table apprehended in moment #2 no longer exists in that moment. It existed the moment before. Since the objects of our consciousnesses are causes of those consciousnesses, and since causes always exist before their effects, most Buddhist systems hold that each consciousness perceives an object that existed in the instant prior to it. Thus, consciousnesses are different entities from their objects in part because they do not exist at the same moment with them.

In contrast, the Mind Only system holds that consciousnesses and their objects arise simultaneously as effects of latencies that have ripened in the mind-basis-of-all. The blue table is not an already existent, external cause that helps to generate a consciousness in the next moment. Rather, the blue table and the consciousness perceiving the blue table are two factors of a single, simultaneous effect. Every consciousness is one substantial entity (*rdzas gcig*) or one entity (*ngo bo gcig*) with its object. This means that they are inextricably linked, each being indispensable to the other. They are not identical, but they are always found together.

To say that an object is one entity with its apprehending consciousness is not to say that it is a consciousness (which is defined as "that which is clear and knowing"). If a blue table were a consciousness, then it would have to be clear and knowing. It would be able to cognize objects of its own, and so forth. Thus, "mind only" does not mean that only consciousnesses, and no forms, exist; it does not mean that only subjects, and no objects, exist. Rather, the point is that objects and their subjects arise together, simultaneously, in a single entity.

We have noted how different this is from other Buddhist views of the relationship between subject and object, but consider how even more dramatically it differs from our ordinary, non-philosophical sense of how things exist. While the ordinary person may never reflect on whether consciousnesses arise after their objects or at the same time with them, it is undeniable that objects appear to us as distant and cut off. We are over here, the blue table is "out there," over there on the other side of the room. It certainly does not appear to be one entity with my mind. If objects and subjects are actually one entity, then why do they so consistently and persistently appear otherwise?

Some say that sentient beings have certain seeds that, in ripening, add an erroneous appearance of subject and object as different entities to whatever else we experience. Things appear distant and cut off today in part because they arise from seeds left by earlier consciousnesses to which things appeared distant and cut off. Things have been appearing this way beginninglessly, and, unlike Christianity, Buddhism provides no story about how things went awry in the absolute beginning.

In any case, it is clear that it is not just a matter of how things appear to our sense consciousnesses. We routinely and innately give our assent to this erroneous appearance of objects and subjects as separate entities. We strongly believe that there is a real, external world that exists apart from our minds. The consciousness that assents to the appearance of an object and its apprehending subject as different entities is, according to the Mind Only system, the most subtle and pernicious form of ignorance—it is the deepest root of cyclic existence. All of the afflictions that hold us in cyclic existence are built on the assent to the mistaken appearance of things as distant and cut off from their apprehenders.

The non-existence of a difference of entity between subject and object is an ultimate truth, an emptiness; it is the subtlest and most profound emptiness that is realized on the path. In order to open us to the idea that there may be no external objects, Asaṅga and his followers adduce examples, taken from sūtra, of situations in which cognition occurs despite the absence of an external object. We know, for example, that in dreams we see objects that seem to exist externally. Through our misapprehension of dream objects as real external phenomena we are drawn into desire, hatred, fear, jealousy, etc. In fact, dream objects do not exist apart from the consciousness apprehending them, but this does not prevent our apprehension of them as distant and cut off, nor our generation of afflictive emotions regarding them. Thus, that the objects of our waking consciousness are associated with different types of reactions and seem to be external does not prove that they actually exist apart from our consciousnesses.

This analogy between waking life and dream life does not imply that waking objects and dream objects are exactly the same. The Mind Only system, like other Buddhist tenet systems, does make a distinction between dreaming and waking life. The objects that appear to us while we are under the influence of sleep are not actually able to perform the functions that they appear to perform: e.g., a dream cup does not hold real water, a dream gun does not shoot real bullets. For the Mind Only system, real bullets are bullets that, while not existing apart from the mind apprehending them, can actually function to kill another being. Actions that we take with regard to dream persons and dream objects do not have the same karmic force of our waking actions. To dream of committing murder is not the same as committing murder. Suppose I dream of murdering someone and, in the dream, the person falls over and stops breathing. This is a dream because there is no corresponding experience, in the continuum of another sentient being, of being murdered and going on to another life.

This discussion shows quite clearly that the Mind Only system is not a form of solipsism. There are other beings whom I may help or harm, love or kill. No object exists apart from the consciousness apprehending it, but there are an infinite number of separate conscious-nesses. This helps the Mind Only proponent deal with the old riddle, "If a tree falls in the forest and no one hears it, is there any sound?" No tree falls, or even exists, apart from consciousness. There are no forests "out there." The witnessing consciousness and the falling tree arise simultaneously as effects of ripened latencies in the continuums of the beings for whom the forest is the "common" environment. If there are no humans, animals, or insects to witness a tree falling, then there must be some type of invisible sentient being, such as a hungry ghost (*yi dwags, preta*).

This assertion of separate consciousnesses, each of which is one entity with its own object, leads to a set of difficult problems that are peculiar to the Mind Only system. If you and I have separate minds, and if every object I see is one entity with my mind and every object you see is one entity with your mind, then how can we have shared objects? How can we sit in a room together and have a conversation? The walls and furniture that you see are one entity with your consciousness and arise from your karma; the walls and furniture I see are one entity with my consciousness and arise from my karma. That has to mean that there are two rooms: one that is with your mind and one that is with my mind. Why is it that both of us see a medium-size room with a rug, two chairs, and red walls?

The Mind Only system holds that our separate minds apprehend, in a more or less synchronized way, very similar apparently external worlds. We are simultaneously creating very similar worlds because each individual possesses a vast number latencies that are very similar to the latencies possessed by other individuals of the same type. The ripening of this "collective karma" creates the appearance that there is just one shared world existing "out there," apart from our minds. We might call this the "common" environment. Although it is not actually a dream (we are not asleep, our actions have moral effects, etc.), the "common" environment is somewhat like a dream that we are all dreaming at the same time.

Of course we are not experiencing exactly the same "dream." There are obviously some differences in the way we perceive things in our "common" environment—differences in the shape (angle of perspective and apparent distance) and color of the visual objects, for example. From a Mind Only point of view, these differences point to the non-existence of a shared external world. The worlds we see are generally alike because we have so many similar latencies, but the ripening of unique, individual latencies also contributes to what we experience. We superimpose additional individual factors, not shared by others, on to the "common" environment.

Many problems and issues remain: What kind of latencies cause us to see each other's bodies—shared, or individual? How does clairvoyance work in a system that holds that my consciousness is separate from yours, but that object and subject are one entity? How does the path work? How does a buddha's mind work? What is the nature of this "mind-basis-of-all"? We do not have room to go into these issues, and it seems inevitable that this brief discussion of Mind Only will raise many doubts and questions.

These problems should be pursued. They should be explored within a spirit of seeking to know the truth about how things exist, not merely out of prejudice against Mind Only as a "lower" tenet system. It is all too easy, out of superficial partisanship for the Middle Way Consequence system, to raise one or two qualms about the Mind Only refutation of external objects and then dismiss the system out of hand. Some of us may have a tendency to want to "jump over" the Mind Only system, saying, "Since the Middle Way Consequence system affirms an external world, I affirm it too." The result can be adding new artificial reinforcement to our innate misconception that there are external objects that truly exist.

That the mind has great power over objects, and is intimately in-
volved with them, is a vital message of the Mind Only system. Another name for the Mind Only system is the Yogic Practice system
(*yogācāra*). This name points to the fact that Mind Only ideas probably
derive, in part, from the experiences of advanced meditators. When
cultivating calm abiding (*zhi gnas, śamatha*), for example, it is said that
one develops a sense of piercing or penetrating the object of one's
concentration. Also, when one realizes emptiness with direct perception, the sense of subject and object as different utterly vanishes. Perhaps this led to the Mind Only assertion that emptiness is the lack of
difference of entity between subject and object. Because it does not
posit an independent solid world of objects apart from consciousness,
Mind Only is a worldview that readily accounts for yogic experiences
such as walking through walls. Yet the Middle Way Consequence system does not give less power to the mind—it gives more. Unlike the
Mind Only system, which holds that the great power of yogic minds
over the world can be explained only by positing objects as one entity
with their apprehenders, the Middle Way Consequence system holds
that the mind is so powerful that it can effect and change an external
world. There is a famous story that Candrakīrti, one of the main teachers of the Middle Way Consequence system, personally demonstrated
the connection between the mind and the external world by milking a
painting of a cow.[28]

The Three Natures

The Mind Only system is presented mainly from the viewpoint of
Buddha's teaching that all phenomena have three natures (*rang bzhin
gsum, trisvabhāva*): thoroughly established (*yongs grub, parinispanna*),
other-powered (*gzhan dbang, paratantra*), and imputational (*kun btags,
parikalpita*). However, there are also presentations of the two truths in
the Mind Only system. Ultimate truths correspond to thoroughly established natures. Conventional truths include other-powered natures
and existent imputational natures. Non-existent imputational natures,
because they do not exist and are not objects of knowledge, are not
included within the two truths.

The three natures (like the two truths) can be posited with regard to
every phenomenon. However, the simplest (and most important) case is
the explanation of the three natures in an other-powered phenomenon,

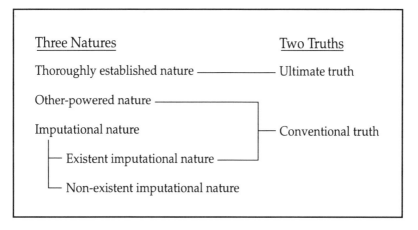

such as a cup. A cup's emptiness of being a different entity from the consciousness apprehending it is its most profound thoroughly established nature. The cup itself is an other-powered nature. The cup's being a different entity from the consciousness apprehending it is its most important imputational nature. Of course, in the Mind Only system a cup is actually not a different entity from the consciousness apprehending it. The cup has this imputational nature only in the sense that it is falsely imputed, or imagined, to have it by an ignorant consciousness of a sentient being.

Among imputational natures, there are two types: existent imputational natures and non-existent imputational natures. We can name an endless number of non-existent imputational natures, such as the horns of rabbit, a real number that is the root of a negative, etc. The most important non-existent imputational natures are those that we habitually and mistakenly imagine to exist: subject and object that are different entities, objects that are established by way of their own character as the referents of their names, and substantially existent persons. (The latter two will be discussed below.) These non-existent imputational natures do not exist at all. They are only mistakenly imagined to exist and therefore, like the horns of a rabbit, they are neither conventional truths nor ultimate truths. Whatever is either of the two truths must exist; whatever is neither of the two truths cannot exist.

Existent imputational natures are permanent phenomena that, like unproduced space, are not among ultimate truths. Existent imputational natures include general or abstract phenomena that do exist (*yod*), but do not truly exist (*bden par yod*) or ultimately exist (*don dam par yod*). They are not produced from causes and conditions. They are called imputational natures because they do not exist by way of their own character, and are imputed by terms and conceptual thought.

Other-powered, or dependent, natures include all impermanent phenomena—tables, chairs, one's body, etc. The Mind Only system holds that other-powered natures are truly and ultimately existent because, unlike imputational natures, they are produced from causes and conditions. Impermanent phenomena are also called "other-powered natures" because they do not sustain themselves from one moment to the next. They arise upon the aggregation of specific sets of causes and conditions, and they change and disintegrate moment by moment. For example, my body exists in this moment under the influence of causes and conditions, including its former moments, that have now ceased and no longer exist. When those causes and conditions came together, a moment of my body arose. Now, lacking any power of its own to continue to a second moment, my body disintegrates. The bodies we have today are obviously different from those we had fifteen or twenty years ago, but those changes happen, not in birthday-by-birthday blocks, but every instant, unnoticed.

Thoroughly established natures are the two selflessnesses—selflessness of persons and selflessness of phenomena. Both are ultimate truths. A selflessness of persons is a person's emptiness of being a substantially existent self. Substantially existent (*rdzas yod*) here means "self-sufficient," i.e., able to set itself up and operate as the controller of mind and body. The selflessness of persons is the coarser and easier to realize of the two selflessnesses, and (according to the Mind Only system) it is the main object realized on a Lesser Vehicle path.

The Mind Only system holds that the mind-basis-of-all is the actual person—the self that is found to exist when it is sought—because it is the entity that transmigrates from one lifetime to the next. The person is imputed to the mental and physical aggregates, but when one searches among those aggregates one does find something—the mind-basis-of-all—that is the actual self. However, a mind-basis-of-all is not a self-sufficient, substantially existent self because it cannot operate, in fact does not exist, apart from the aggregates. Nonetheless, the mind-basis-of-all is mistakenly apprehended as a self-sufficient self. Recall that the Mind Only system posits—in addition to the mind-basis-of-all, the five sense consciousnesses, and the mental consciousness—a special mind called afflicted mentality (*yid nyon, kliṣṭamanas*). The conception of a substantially existent self arises because afflicted mentality observes the mind-basis-of-all and wrongly takes it to be a substantially existent self.

As for the selflessness of phenomena, the absence of a difference of entity between subject and object is the subtlest and most profound nature of all phenomena. This is the main object of realization of a bodhisattva path. Through meditating upon this emptiness, bodhisattvas are able not only to escape cyclic existence, but also to achieve omniscience.

There is another, related selflessness of phenomena: the non-existence of phenomena by way of their own character as the referents of names. This is said to be just as subtle as, but easier to realize than, the non-existence of subject and object as different entities. The relationship between the two selflessnesses of phenomena deserves some further attention.

Language and Reference

Like all other Buddhist tenet systems, the Mind Only system holds that names are arbitrary and conventional, differing from one language to another. There is more than just this in the Mind Only system's assertion that phenomena do not exist by way of their own character as the referents of names.

We can approach this assertion by comparing it to the teachings of the Sūtra system. In the Sūtra system, each term has two referent objects: (1) the internal generic meaning-image (*don spyi*) and (2) the object itself. The internal image is the main referent in the sense that it has the most immediate and primary connection with the term. It is through such images that we speak and hear. The actual object is the secondary referent—a term does "get at it," but only via the generic image. The actual object, unlike the generic images, can be an impermanent phenomenon, a phenomenon that (according to the Sūtra system) exists by way of its own character. Thus, the proponents of the Sūtra system clearly understand that the primary referent of a term (the meaning-image) is not in the nature of the actual object. However, the secondary referent of a term is the actual external object.

Proponents of the Mind Only system, denying the existence of objects external to the consciousness apprehending them, take the analysis of terms and their referents one step farther. They distinguish the mere appearance of a flag, for example, from the mistaken appearance of the flag as being established by way of its character as the referent of the name "flag." When we think "flag," the primary referent is the mental image of a flag. The secondary referent is an actual object, a flag, that we mistakenly imagine as existing "out there"—external, distant, and cut off from our consciousnesses.

The Sūtra system says that there is a flag out there, apart from the mind, to which the term "flag" is referring. That flag out there is the secondary referent of the term "flag." The Mind Only system, on the other hand, denies that such a secondary referent is established by way of its own character in the nature of the flag. That is, there is no flag that exists on its own, apart from the mind apprehending it, as the basis of the name "flag." When something appears to be established by way of its own character as the referent of a name, it appears as though it were, by nature, a different entity from the consciousness that is "referring" to it, i.e., apprehending it. Thus, there is a close relationship between the two selflessnesses of phenomena in the Mind Only system. Meditation on how phenomena are not established by way of their own character as the referents of names is a good way to approach realization of the non-existence of subject and object as different entities.

It is not just conceptual consciousnesses that are affected by the false appearance of phenomena as established by way of their own character as the referents of names. The raw (pre-conceptual) appearance of a flag to an eye consciousness is already mixed with an appearance of the flag as established by way of its own character as the referent of a name. Proponents of Mind Only say that there is a seed that produces the appearance of a flag, another seed that produces its appearance as a different entity from the consciousness apprehending it, and a third simultaneously ripening seed that produces the flag's appearance as established by way of its own character as the referent of its name.

The mistaken appearance and mistaken conception that phenomena are established by way of their own character as the referents of names occurs even with regard to newly encountered phenomena for which we have no names. Without a name for something, we already have a sense of its being naturally suitable to be the basis of a name. Thus, the ignorant apprehension of phenomena as established by way of their own character as the referents of names affects every sentient being—even those, such as animals and babies, who do not use terminology.

The Two Truths

In Great Vehicle tenet systems, the term "truth" (*bden pa, satya*) refers to something that exists just as it appears and appears just as it exists; it is non-deceptive (*mi slu ba*). When something is a truth, its mode of appearance coincides with its mode of existence. A falsity (*rdzun pa*), on the other hand, is something that appears in one way and exists in another way. This usage is comparable to the distinction we make between a true friend and false friend. Both appear to be friends, but only one is actually a friend.

Great Vehicle tenet systems hold that only ultimate truths are truths; all conventional truths are falsities. In the Mind Only system, emptiness (the non-existence of external objects) is a truth because it exists as it appears for the meditative consciousness that directly realizes it. On the other hand, a conventional truth, such as a cup, is a falsity because it appears to exist as a different entity from the consciousness apprehending it, but actually exists as one entity with the consciousness apprehending it. Conventional truths falsely appear to us as distant and cut off.

If cups and so forth are actually falsities, then why are they called conventional truths (*kun rdzob bden pa, saṃvṛti-satya*)? According to Jangya (lCang skya) and Ngawang Palden, conventional truths are so-called because they exist in the perspective, or through the force, of conventional designations, expressions, and consciousnesses.[29] Thus, they hold that within the term "conventional truth," the word "truth" merely indicates that something exists, and does not refer to something that exists as it appears.

However, Jamyang Shayba gives a different etymology of the term *kun rdzob bden pa*, which we have been translating as "conventional truth" Jamyang Shayba indicates that *kun rdzob bden pa* means "truth for the perspective of an ignorant consciousness that conceals the real nature of phenomena." (This etymology is shared by all Great Vehicle tenet systems, and accordingly we shall hereafter translate *kun rdzob bden pa* as "truth-for-a-concealer" or "concealer-truth.") A cup is not a truth because it does not exist as it appears. It is mistaken for a truth by a consciousness that conceals the way that things actually exist,

preventing us from seeing reality. In the Mind Only system, the ignorant consciousness for which a cup is a truth is a consciousness that
sees subject and object as different entities. Only such a consciousness
would take a cup to be something that exists as it appears.

Thus, the term *kun rdzob bden pa* works rather like the term "fool's
gold." Fool's gold is not gold at all—it is something that is mistaken for
gold by a fool. In India, one of my Tibetan teachers offered a more pun-
gent example: It is like saying that something (e.g., garbage or excrement)
smells good to a dog.[30] This is not intended to suggest that it actually
smells good—quite to the contrary. Likewise, the very term "truth-
for-a-concealer" or "concealer-truth" (*kun rdzob bden pa*) is intended to
generate dissatisfaction with the way things ordinarily appear.

Selflessnesses, the thoroughly established natures, are called ultimate truths because they are realized by an ultimate mind. Here, an
ultimate mind is a mind that realizes the highest object of a particular path to liberation. Some critics of Buddhism have confused this
ultimate mind with the ultimate state (*go 'phang*) that is attained on
the path. Subject and object are not differentiated for the ultimate
mind directly realizing emptiness, and nothing other than emptiness appears to or is realized by that ultimate mind. Hearing this,
some have taken Buddhism to be a quest for a trance-like withdrawal
from the world of appearances into solitary tranquility. Actually, the
Great Vehicle tenet systems clearly indicate that the ultimate state is
buddha-hood—a state wherein, having trained in meditations on
both conventional truths and ultimate truths, one is at last able to
see all conventional phenomena (including other people) from within
meditative equipoise on emptiness. This is not the end of one's relationships with sentient beings, but the perfection of those relationships in spontaneous, perfectly clear-eyed love.

The definitions of the two truths in the Mind Only system are not
among the most illuminating definitions, and thus we have not built
our discussion around them. Still, they are certainly worth our attention. Gönchok Jikme Wangpo (dKon mchog 'jigs med dbang po)
defines an ultimate truth as:

> an object found by a correct knower which distinguishes an ulti-
> mate object

and defines a conventional truth as:

> an object found by a correct knower which is a valid cognizer dis-
> tinguishing a conventionality.[31]

These definitions point to the fact that the two truths are two classes of existent objects that are mutually exclusive and which are "found" (*rnyed*) or realized by two different types of correct knowledge. Although conventional truths appear to sentient beings in a deceptive way, they do exist and are cognized even by buddhas.

Other definitions, given by Jangya and Ngawang Palden, revolve around the fact that a sentient being's direct realization of an ultimate truth can work as an antidote to an obstruction (either an afflictive obstruction or an obstruction to omniscience) in that sentient being's continuum.[32] Unlike a conventional truth, an ultimate truth is the most important thing that is realized on a path leading to liberation. Realization of the selflessness of persons is the key to the attainment of liberation on a Lesser Vehicle path, while realization of the selflessness of phenomena is the key to enlightenment on the bodhisattva path.

The Middle Way and Mind Only Systems

Among proponents of the Middle Way system, there are a variety of opinions about the Mind Only doctrine. The most sympathetic are scholars of the Yogic Practice division of the Autonomy subsystem of the Middle Way system (e.g., Śāntirakṣita and Kamalaśīla). They accept the non-existence of a difference of entity between subject and object, but posit this as a coarse selflessness of phenomena.

The least sympathetic is Bhāvaviveka, founder of the Sūtric division of the Autonomy subsystem of the Middle Way system. He claims that Buddha never in any way denied the existence of external objects. According to Bhāvaviveka's *Blaze of Reasoning*, the Mind Only doctrine was "shamelessly" fabricated by Asaṅga and his followers based on complete misinterpretations of certain sūtra passages.[33] For example, Bhāvaviveka argues that neither the statement in the *Descent into Laṅkā Sūtra*, "External appearances do not exist," nor the statement in the *Sūtra on the Ten Grounds*, "These three realms are mind only," is in any way intended to refute external objects. Bhāvaviveka contends that the true and literal import of these passages is that there are no agents of actions or experiencers of the karmic effects that exist apart from the mind. As falsifications of the authentic teaching of Buddha, Mind Only doctrines have no value, even provisionally. Bhāvaviveka's *Lamp for Wisdom* states that to first hold Mind Only tenets and later give them up for the Middle Way view "is like first anointing oneself with mud and then later bathing; better to keep one's distance from the beginning."[34]

Candrakīrti, founder of the Middle Way Consequence system—the "highest rung" on the Gelukpa "ladder" of tenets—strongly differs with Bhāvaviveka. Candrakīrti and his followers say that Buddha did teach Mind Only doctrine, but did not hold it as his own final view. Candrakīrti cites the *Descent into Laṅkā Sūtra*:[35]

> Just as a physician gives medicines
> To a patient for illness,
> So the buddhas teach
> Mind Only to sentient beings.

Although external objects do exist, the Buddha taught the non-existence of external objects for the sake of reducing attachment to what appear to be inherently existent (*rang bzhin gyis grub pa, svabhāvasiddha*) external forms. In the Middle Way Consequence system, external objects exist conventionally, but neither minds nor their objects exist inherently. The emptiness of inherent existence is the ultimate truth that must be realized on a path to liberation. For some trainees, the easiest approach to realization of emptiness is via realization that there are no inherently existent external forms. Even though external objects do exist conventionally, the Buddha denied external objects for the sake of helping certain trainees to reduce their attachment to these apparently real external forms. Thus, for many, the Mind Only system is not an unnecessary mud-bath, but an invaluable stepping-stone to the Middle Way view.

For the sake of helping others, Buddha spoke words that are not literally true, but in teaching that there are no external objects and that all is "mind only," Buddha conveyed a key truth: mind is the principal creator of everything. By training our minds in ethics, meditative stabilization, and wisdom, we gradually gain control over the type of bodies and environments we are creating. Finally, each of us will create a pure land and become a buddha.

Proponents of the Middle Way Consequence system do not regard the refutation of external objects as literally acceptable. They argue that consciousnesses and their external objects are interdependent—neither exists without the other. Thus, if there were no external objects there would be no consciousnesses. The externality of objects is a legitimate conventional understanding of the world. Unlike the perception of objects as inherently existent, the perception of objects as external is not refuted by yogic analysis. Like everything that exists at all, external objects exist in conventional terms (*tha snyad du yod*).

On the other hand, the Middle Way Consequence system supports the Mind Only position that there are no inherently existent external objects. Since our ordinary sense of existence is thoroughly entangled with a sense of inherent existence, when we affirm external objects from within our ordinary sense of how things exist we do not surpass the Mind Only view, but fall far below it. We add new artificial reinforcement to the innate misapprehension of external objects as inherently existent.

Chapter Six
The Middle Way System

Nāgārjuna pioneered the Middle Way system, arguing in his *Treatise on the Middle Way* and other works that the meaning of Buddha's teaching of emptiness, the ultimate truth, is that when one analytically searches for things that seem real, they are not findable. Therefore, there is nothing that is truly or ultimately existent. Jamyang Shayba gives a general definition of a proponent of the Middle Way system:

> A proponent of Buddhist tenets who totally refutes all extremes of permanence, i.e., that any phenomenon ultimately exists, and refutes all extremes of annihilation, i.e., that phenomena do not exist conventionally.[36]

An extreme of permanence is any position that reifies phenomena, attributing to them a type of existence that they lack. An extreme of annihilation is any position that deprecates phenomena by denying a type of existence that does occur.

Actually, every system of Buddhist tenets claims to chart the middle way between the extremes of permanence and annihilation, and each system regards other Buddhist and non-Buddhist systems as falling to extreme views. Broadly speaking, as we move up the Geluk ladder of tenets, we find that what each system denies—against the extreme of permanence—is more and more, while what each system affirms—against the extreme of annihilation—is less and less.

The Great Exposition system avoids the extreme of permanence by asserting that all compounded phenomena disintegrate moment by moment, while avoiding the extreme of annihilation by asserting that everything is substantially established (*rdzas grub, dravya-siddha*). The Great Exposition system alone distinguishes substantial establishment from substantial existence (*rdzas yod, dravya-sat*). Only ultimate truths (e.g., partless particles and partless moments of consciousness) substantially exist, but all phenomena are substantially established in the sense that they have their own autonomous substance.[37] In the Great Exposition system there is a strong sense that everything must have its own "substance" in order to exist at all.

The Followers of Reasoning within the Sūtra system move a step away from this sense of substantiality (an extreme of permanence) by holding that some existents (e.g., permanent phenomena and the person) are only imputedly existent (*btags yod, prajñapti-sat*). This means that it is possible for some things to exist without having their own substance, without being entirely autonomous entities. Persons, for example, are imputed by conceptual thought upon the apprehension of the psycho-physical aggregates. Meanwhile, the Sūtra system avoids the extreme of annihilation by asserting that all phenomena are established by way of their own character as the referents or bases of words and conceptuality.

Proponents of the Mind Only system avoid the extreme of permanence by refuting part of what the Sūtra system affirms—the existence of phenomena by way of their own character as the referents of terms and conceptuality. They avoid the extreme of annihilation by holding that all ultimate truths are ultimately established, existing by way of their own nature, and that impermanent conventional truths must be "truly existent" inasmuch as they are actually produced from causes and conditions.

Finally, the Middle Way system, regarding all of the lower systems as falling mainly to the extreme of permanence, avoids that extreme by asserting that there is nothing that is truly or ultimately existent. It avoids the extreme of annihilation by asserting that phenomena do exist conventionally. Since everything that exists exists only conventionally, and nothing exists ultimately, it is important (1) not to confuse ultimate existence (*don dam par yod pa*) with ultimate truth (*don dam bden pa*), and (2) not to confuse conventional existence (*kun rdzob tu yod pa*) with conventional truth or concealer-truth (*kun rdzob bden pa*). Remember that in all of these systems the two truths are objects of knowledge, existents. In the Middle Way system, the two truths both exist conventionally; neither exists ultimately.

Still, since emptiness (ultimate truth) is the quality of lacking ultimate existence, knowing an ultimate truth entails knowing how to refute the exaggerated type of existence (ultimate existence) that we ignorantly superimpose on the world. Similarly, to understand concealer-truths means to know how persons, actions, and their effects, and the other varieties of conventional phenomena do exist conventionally. Therefore, the two truths are used as a framework for explaining how things exist without truly or ultimately existing.

Chapter Seven
The Autonomy System

Tibetan scholars divide the Middle Way system into the Autonomy system (*rang rgyud pa, svātantrika*) and the Consequence system (*thal 'gyur pa, prāsaṅgika*). However, these terms do not appear in Indian literature as names for two distinct subsystems. They were probably coined by Tibetan scholars in the eleventh century, after the works of Candrakīrti had been translated. Noting Candrakīrti's emphasis on logical consequences and his sharp attack on Bhāvaviveka, they designated Candrakīrti and his followers "Consequentialists" and called Bhāvaviveka and his supporters "Autonomists." These terms refer to conflicting positions on how proponents of the Middle Way should frame arguments against their opponents. Bhāvaviveka apparently felt that one must use syllogisms (*sbyor ba, prayoga*), or else consequences (*thal 'gyur, prasaṅga*) that will eventually be followed by syllogisms. Bhāvaviveka criticized Buddhapālita's commentary on Nāgārjuna's *Treatise on the Middle Way,* arguing that Buddhapālita's logical method was faulty because he mainly relied upon contradictory consequences—i.e., arguments of the *reductio ad absurdum* type—that did not convert into appropriate syllogistic demonstrations. Candrakīrti defended Buddhapālita, arguing that a proponent of the Middle Way is not required to construct arguments that conclude in syllogisms.

It was Tsong Khapa who first argued that the Autonomy/Consequence distinction is a difference not only in logical method but in philosophical view as well. Tsong Khapa showed that Bhāvaviveka's insistence upon the eventual use of syllogisms implies that the terms of debate (subjects, etc.) "appear in common" to both parties, i.e., that the systems of both parties implicitly or explicitly accept that the consciousnesses that certify the terms of debate also certify the inherent existence of the terms of debate. From this, Tsong Khapa deduced that Bhāvaviveka, unlike Candrakīrti, accepts that phenomena do exist in accordance with their appearance as inherently existent (*rang bzhin gyis grub pa, svabhāvasiddha*), that is, existent by way of their own character (*rang gi mtshan nyid kyis grub pa, svalakṣaṇasiddha*).

Accordingly, a proponent of the Middle Way Autonomy system is someone who refutes true existence and ultimate existence (thus avoiding the extreme of permanence) but asserts that all phenomena inherently exist in a conventional sense (thus avoiding the extreme of annihilation). A Consequentialist, on the other hand, denies that phenomena inherently exist even conventionally (thus avoiding the extreme of permanence), but does admit the mere conventional existence of phenomena (thus avoiding the extreme of annihilation).

For Autonomists, an emptiness of true existence is an ultimate truth. This emptiness is a subtle selflessness of phenomena, i.e., the most profound object to be realized on the bodhisattva path. Emptiness of ultimate existence and emptiness of true existence are two names for the same thing. Thus, in order to understand what an ultimate truth is for the Autonomy system, we must first understand how something would exist if it were truly or ultimately existent. We can then understand ultimate truth as the absence of such true or ultimate existence in phenomena.

Ultimate Existence

What would it mean to be truly or ultimately existent? Bhāvaviveka's *Blaze of Reasoning* suggests that ultimate existence means being able to stand up under analysis by an ultimate mind. An ultimate mind is a consciousness of analytical wisdom that searches out the way that things exist, their final mode of being. If something were ultimately existent, it would exist for and be found by the reasoning consciousness analyzing its final mode of being. That is, if a chair were truly existent, then when I search to see how a chair really exists I should at last find the chair itself. Instead, Bhāvaviveka explains, the mind searching for the final nature of the chair finds the emptiness of the chair, that is, the chair's quality of being devoid of true existence.

It is important to distinguish "being found (*rnyed*) by an ultimate mind" from "being able to bear analysis (*dpyad bzod thub pa*) by an ultimate mind." Ultimate truths are found by the ultimate analytical wisdom consciousnesses of sentient beings. On the other hand, nothing at all withstands analysis by an ultimate mind. Failing to make this distinction, certain early Tibetan scholars (e.g., Chaba Chökyi Senge [Phya pa Chos kyi seng ge]) concluded that emptiness must ultimately exist because of existing for an ultimate mind. Others (e.g., Ngok Loden Sherap [rNgog bLo ldan shes rab]), certain that emptiness could not ultimately exist, concluded that emptiness is not knowable because it is found neither by conventional minds nor by ultimate minds that search for it. Tsong Khapa's interpretation is that emptiness is found, known, and realized by a mind of ultimate analysis, and therefore it is an ultimate truth. However, emptiness is not ultimately existent because it is not found by the ultimate mind analyzing emptiness itself. For example, when a chair is the basis of analysis, the ultimate mind finds not the chair but the emptiness of the chair. When the emptiness of the chair is the basis of analysis, the ultimate mind finds not the emptiness of the chair but the emptiness of the emptiness of the chair, and so forth. In other words, an emptiness is no more able to sustain ultimate analysis than anything else. Every emptiness is the final mode of abiding of some phenomenon (either an ultimate truth or a concealer-truth), but no emptiness is its own final mode of abiding.

Thus, according to the Geluk reading of Bhāvaviveka, ultimate existence would entail that something exist as its own final nature, while the emptiness of a phenomenon points to its inability to hold up under analysis of its final nature. However, in his retrospective formulation of the view of the Autonomy system, Tsong Khapa determines that the ignorance imagining that something can sustain ultimate analysis of its nature is artificial ignorance, an idea arising under the influence of training in the wrong tenets of other systems. This way of thinking about ultimate existence does not arise innately.

In order to find the main meaning of ultimate existence in the Autonomy system, that is, in order to identify the mistaken sense of ultimate existence that arises innately as the root of suffering in cyclic existence, Tsong Khapa turns to a later Indian proponent of the Autonomy Middle Way system. From a passage by Kamalaśīla, Tsong Khapa deduces that ultimate existence (if it were possible) would be an object's quality of existing by way of its own uncommon mode of subsistence without relying on being posited by way of appearing to a non-defective awareness. The conventional status of objects is that they do exist by way of their own mode of subsistence, but only in reliance upon appearing to a non-defective mind. A non-defective awareness is a sense or mental consciousness that is not affected by either superficial or deep causes of error. Superficial causes of error are non-innate, temporary circumstances that cause a mistaken perception or idea—e.g., reflections, echoes, mirages, taking drugs, studying lower tenet systems, etc. Deep sources of error are innate misconceptions, such as the ignorant conception of things as ultimately existent. Phenomena are not posited through their appearance to such mistaken consciousnesses, but through their appearance to correct consciousnesses.

The Magic Show

Perhaps a consideration of the traditional "magic show" analogy can afford some insight into this explanation of how things exist by way of their own characters conventionally, but not ultimately. First, we will give the analogy, then give a brief explanation of it in terms of the general view of the Middle Way system, and finally elaborate how the analogy can be used to explain the view of the Autonomy system.

Suppose that a magician, by applying a special salve and reciting a mantra, causes a small rock to appear as an elephant. The spell works by affecting both the stone and the visual faculties of anyone present, the spectators as well as the magician. Everyone present when the mantra and salve are applied sees what appears to be an actual elephant. The spectators mistake this illusory elephant for a real elephant. Some of them worry that the elephant might be dangerous, a few are jealous of the magician who is in possession of such a marvelous beast, while others are wondering if they might be able to buy or borrow the elephant for a festival or to help clear a new field. The magician also sees the appearance of an elephant, but unlike the spectators he recognizes it as an illusion and thus knows that there is no elephant present. Finally, some spectators arrive late, after the mantra has already been cast. Unlike the magician and the other spectators, these latecomers are not affected by the mantra, and thus they do not see an elephant at all; they see only the stone. However, one of the latecomers is clairvoyant. Like the other latecomers, when he looks at the stone he sees a stone; he does not mistake it for an elephant. But at the same time, because he knows the minds of those who were present when the mantra was cast, he also sees the illusory elephant that is appearing to them.

Thus, this analogy involves a stone, an elephant, and at least four people: (1) the ordinary spectator (who sees an elephant and believes it to be real), (2) the magician (who sees the elephant but knows that it is an illusion), (3) the latecomer (who sees only a stone) and (4) the clairvoyant latecomer (who sees only the stone from his own viewpoint, but also sees the elephant as something that is appearing to the other minds).[38] The stone represents phenomena without the overlay of true existence. The elephant represents these same phenomena, but with the overlay of true existence. The ordinary spectator—who sees the elephant, believes that it is real, and thus falls prey to fear, greed, envy, etc.—is like the ordinary sentient being who, when perceiving phenomena, mistakenly believes that they truly exist, and thus is trapped in cyclic existence. The latecomer who sees only the stone is like a buddha because a buddha's mind is completely unaffected by error. In another way, the clairvoyant latecomer who sees both the stone (from his own perspective) and the elephant (through seeing what appears to others) is also like an omniscient buddha who sees all deceptive and non-deceptive phenomena, all concealer-truths and ultimate truths. The magician can be compared to an *arhat* who has overcome the ignorant conception of the substantial existence of persons, and is thus not drawn into afflictive emotions despite perceiving phenomena as truly existent.

Now, let us consider how this analogy helps us to understand the Autonomy system's position that emptiness of ultimate existence means something's lack of existing by way of its own uncommon mode of subsistence without being posited through appearing to a non-defective mind. The appearance of the stone as an elephant arises because the mind of the spectator is affected by the mantra—otherwise, a stone would appear. On the other hand, the casting of the mantra also affects the stone. While an ordinary stone has no quality that causes it to appear as an elephant, a stone that has been conjured with salve and mantra gains an additional and distinctive objective status that allows it to appear as an elephant. In casting the mantra on the stone, it is as though the magician were painting an image of an elephant on a three-dimensional canvas. Without this appearance of the stone as an elephant, the spectators would never mistake it for a real elephant. The stone does not appear as an elephant from its own side without depending on the mind—but the stone has an uncommon mode of being which appears as an elephant. The elephant can be posited only in reliance upon its appearance to the mind affected by the mantra, but it is not a baseless fabrication or projection.

Analogously, the Autonomy system holds that two factors contribute to the way that things conventionally exist: (1) the objective mode of subsistence or character of the object and (2) the appearance of the object to a conceptual or non-conceptual awareness that is non-defective. Neither of these factors is alone sufficient to posit the object's existence. Without its own objective status a phenomenon could never appear to a non-defective awareness. Thus, from an Autonomist perspective, the Consequentialists fall to an extreme of annihilation by denying that tables, chairs, persons, actions, etc. have their own character even conventionally. Autonomists insist that there has to be an objectively established basis for things. If one sees an elephant when one looks at an ordinary stone on which no mantra has been cast, or if one sees a tiger when looking at a blank canvas, then that elephant or tiger is entirely unreal and fictitious. If all phenomena were posited in an analogous manner, as mere mental constructions with no input from the object's own character, then (say the Autonomists) there would no way to posit the definite links between actions and their karmic effects, no way to posit persons as the agents of actions and the experiencers of their effects, no way to posit the path, and so forth.

On the other hand, Autonomists hold that a phenomenon gets its entity through the power of the non-defective awareness to which it appears. A painting of a tiger does not independently appear as a tiger; it appears as a tiger in relation to the mind apprehending the painting. Analogously, phenomena have their own uncommon mode of subsistence, but that mode of subsistence depends upon their appearance to a correct consciousness. If they had their own way of existing even without appearing to a non-defective consciousness, then they would be ultimately existent. To assert (as do the lower tenet systems) that some (or all) phenomena ultimately exist is to fall to an extreme of permanence. In addition to conceptions of ultimate existence acquired through the study of tenets, there is also an innate ignorance conceiving ultimate existence which is the root of suffering in cyclic existence. This ignorance is a conceptual consciousness apprehending its object as existing exclusively from its own side—without relying upon its appearance to a non-defective awareness.

Definitions of the Two Truths

Presenting the two truths in the Autonomy system, Ngawang Palden writes:[39]

> The definition of an ultimate truth is: a phenomenon realized by the direct valid cognizer realizing it by way of the vanishing of dualistic appearance. The definition of a concealer-truth is: a phenomenon realized by the direct valid cognizer realizing it by way of an association with dualistic appearance.

Dualistic appearance (*gnyis snang*), according to context, can refer to many different things, including (1) the appearance of a generic meaning-image, (2) the appearance of subject and object, (3) the appearances of true existence, (4) the appearance of difference, and (5) the appearance of any conventional phenomenon. Here, the vanishing of dualistic appearance refers to the vanishing of all types of dualistic appearance. In general, all direct perceivers lack the first type of dualistic appearance because they get at their object directly, not through the appearance of a generic image. Most direct perceivers have several of the other types of dualistic appearance, and some direct perceivers have all of the other types. If a direct perceiver gets at its object via any type of dualistic appearance, then that object must be a concealer-truth.

When a sentient being directly realizes the absence of true existence, all types of dualistic appearance vanish. There is no sense of difference between subject and object and no appearance of any conventional phenomenon. In terms of their final natures, emptiness and the mind realizing emptiness are "of one taste" in being empty of true existence. The experience of realizing emptiness directly has been likened to pouring fresh water into fresh water. Since direct realization of emptiness arises in this totally non-dualistic manner, emptiness is an ultimate truth.

It is also possible to realize emptiness conceptually, with inference. In fact, the Geluk tradition emphasizes that inferential cognition of emptiness is a stepping-stone to direct cognition of emptiness, and Bhāvaviveka's *Blaze of Reasoning* provides evidence to support this view. Thus, these definitions of the two truths do not mean that only direct cognition of emptiness is possible. Rather, the point is that while conceptual consciousnesses are always dualistic, direct perceivers may be dualistic or completely non-dualistic—depending upon whether their object is a concealer-truth or an ultimate truth.

Although Gelukpa scholars disagree on some fine points related to the various definitions of the two truths in the Middle Way system, in general there is nothing to preclude the use of this set of definitions in the Consequentialist system as well as in the Autonomist system. Definitions like these have been used in the Consequentialist system by scholars such as Gyeltsap (rGyal tshab) and Jamyang Shayba. The Consequentialists disagree with the Autonomists over the precise character of emptiness, but they agree that emptiness, when realized directly by a sentient being, is experienced in a state devoid of all dualistic appearance.

A buddha (who, having abandoned all limitations, is no longer classified as a sentient being), continuously and simultaneously realizes all phenomena with all six mental and sense consciousnesses. This means that a buddha has dualistic appearance (with regard to conventional phenomena) at the same time that he/she directly realizes emptiness. However, there is no need to make a buddha's mode of cognition a special exception to these definitions because buddhas realize all ultimate truths by way of a vanishing of dualistic appearance and all concealer-truths by way of an association with dualistic appearance. The dualistic appearance that arises for a buddha in his/her vision of conventionalities does not interfere with the simultaneous but completely non-dualistic vision of emptiness.

Division of Concealer-truths

Autonomists subdivide concealer-truths into real conventionalities (*yang dag kun rdzob, tathya-saṃvṛti*) and unreal conventionalities (*log pa'i kun rdzob, mitya-saṃvṛti*). Jñānagarbha's *Differentiation of the Two Truths*:

> Real and unreal conventionalities are distinguished [respectively]
> By their ability or inability to function as they appear.[40]

A mirage, a reflection, a magician's illusion, etc. are all things that exist and are concealer-truths. However, they mislead the sense consciousnesses to which they appear. They appear to be able to function as water, and so forth, while in fact they cannot, and thus they are posited as unreal conventionalities. On the other hand, water, a face, an elephant, and so forth can actually function just as they appear to ordinary direct perception. They are accordingly classified as real conventionalities.

Sūtric Autonomists and Yogic Autonomists

As this distinction between real and unreal conventionalities suggests, Autonomists (according to Geluk presentations) place great trust in the way things appear to ordinary direct perception. Autonomists (unlike Consequentialists) believe that the raw data of ordinary direct perception is deceptive neither with regard to ultimate existence nor with regard to inherent existence.[41] That is, when my eye consciousness sees a blue chair, the chair appears to be inherently existent and it actually is inherently existent. It does not appear to be ultimately existent, and in fact it is not ultimately existent. The deceptive appearance of things as ultimately existent begins with the arising of mistaken conceptuality. From the first inkling of conceptual recognition, even before I think, "Now I am seeing a blue chair," the chair seems to be ultimately existent, something that can set itself up without depending on the consciousness to which it appears.

Although Autonomists agree among themselves that direct perception has no mistaken appearance of things as ultimately existent,[42] they disagree as to whether such consciousnesses are mistaken with regard to the apparent externality of objects. Bhāvaviveka and his followers are called Sūtric Autonomists because, like proponents of the Sūtra system, they assert inherently existent external objects. As explained above, Bhāvaviveka was quite hostile to the Mind Only position that objects are not different entities from the minds apprehending them. Thus, the Sūtric Autonomists maintain that normal direct perception is not mistaken either with regard to the appearance of external objects or with regard to anything else. Whatever appears to the healthy eyes and ears of the ordinary person does exist, conventionally, just as it appears.

The Yogic branch of the Autonomy system, historically the last of the systems to develop fully, combines Middle Way ideas inherited from Nāgārjuna and Bhāvaviveka with Mind Only ideas inherited from Asaṅga. Although Śāntarakṣita was not the first scholar to adopt such an approach, he is considered the founder of the system because he was the first to elaborate its view systematically. Along with successors such as Kamalaśīla and Jñānagarbha, Śāntarakṣita holds that (1) nothing exists ultimately and (2) even conventionally there are no objects that are different entities from the minds apprehending them. Sharing the general Middle Way view that the emptiness of ultimate existence is the subtle and profound selflessness that must be realized on the bodhisattva path, the Yogic Autonomy Middle Way system treats the non-difference of entity between subject and object as a coarse self-lessness of phenomena. In his *Ornament to the Middle*, Śāntarakṣita pro-poses exactly what Bhāvaviveka had advised against: first using the "mind only" doctrine to refute external objects and thereafter advanc-ing to a refutation of truly existent consciousnesses.

The Mind Only system and the Middle Way system flourished side by side in India, and they had ample opportunity to interact. Some-times this relationship was harmonious, as in the case of scholars (e.g., Asaṅga) who wrote separate treatises within both systems and the case of later scholars (Śāntarakṣita, etc.) who combined ideas from the two to create a new subsystem. On the other hand, partisans on either side did produce refutations of opposing systems.

Among the Middle Way system's criticisms of the Mind Only sys-tem, a central point is that, while undercutting our ignorant reification of external objects, Mind Only tends to reify the mind. We saw that the Great Exposition system considers only what is irreducible to be ultimately existent, and attacks our sense of composite phenomena as unitary and substantial wholes. However, the next rung on the ladder of tenets, the Sūtra system, refuses to consider irreducible parts as any more real than composite wholes. In a somewhat parallel way, the Middle Way system sees the Mind Only system as erroneously tilt-ing toward subjects in its attempts to refute external objects We ordi-narily think that if something does not exist apart from our minds then it could not exist at all. Mind Only seeks to overcome this mis-conception, positing objects that really exist, yet are one entity with consciousness. To speak of this refutation of a difference of entity between subjects and objects as a refutation of external objects—rather than a refutation of internal subjects—opens the Mind Only system to accusations of a bias that gives a special extra-strong kind of reality to consciousnesses, especially the mind-basis-of-all.

In the Middle Way system, wholes depend on parts, but parts also depend on wholes; effects depend on causes, but causes also depend on effects; and objects depend on subjects but subjects also depend on objects. Nothing is what it is autonomously, essentially, ultimately, or independently. Mind still plays a special role in the existence of the world because nothing of any sort is posited except through the route of appearing to a non-defective mind. On the other hand, there is never any sense or implication that consciousnesses are any more real than anything else. Consciousnesses exist not in and of themselves, but only in relation to other phenomena—as knowers of their objects and as objects appearing to other consciousnesses.[43]

Selflessness

We have seen that the Lesser Vehicle tenet systems teach that liberation from cyclic existence requires realization of the person's emptiness of a substantially existent, self-sufficient nature. In addition, the Mind Only and Autonomy systems also agree that this is the subtle personal selflessness that certain Lesser Vehicle practitioners take as their main object of meditation. According to all systems except the Consequentialist, it is possible to achieve liberation from cyclic existence through mainly meditating on the non-existence of a self-sufficient person. There is some controversy among Gelukpas as to whether Autonomists classify the non-existence of a self-sufficient person as an ultimate truth, but the preponderance of evidence favors the view that they do.[44]

Within the Autonomy system, Sūtra Autonomists and Yogic Autonomists disagree regarding the main object of meditation for Solitary Realizers, the other type of Lesser Vehicle practitioner. Sūtra Autonomists again posit the non-existence of a self-sufficient person, but Yogic Autonomists posit the non-difference of entity between an object and the consciousness apprehending it. The Mind Only system regards this emptiness as the subtle selflessness of phenomena that is mainly realized by bodhisattvas, but the Yogic Autonomists regard it as a coarse selflessness of phenomena realized by bodhisattvas as a stepping-stone to the subtle emptiness, but not as their main object of meditation.

The Autonomists all hold that emptiness of ultimate existence is the subtle selflessness of phenomena and the main object of meditation on the bodhisattva path.

Chapter Eight
The Consequence System

Buddhism teaches that we innately and ignorantly imagine persons and things to be more real than they actually are. The various tenet systems agree that the deepest and subtlest form of ignorance is the root of all misery, but they disagree about how deep these roots go. Buddhist practitioners are like surgeons who, though receiving the counsel of senior surgeons, must operate on themselves. They must cut deep enough to get at the source of their disease, the very subtlest ignorance, but not so deep as to damage vital organs—ethics, compassion, the path, buddhahood, etc. A cut too shallow may bring some temporary benefits, but does not cure. A cut too deep leads to the dangerous extreme of nihilism.

The Gelukpa ladder of tenets ascends through a series of refinements in describing "how deep to cut," i.e., what kind of self must be refuted and what kind of ignorance must be abandoned in order to reach perfect health. At the top of the ladder, the Consequentialists argue for the deepest cut into our accustomed way of seeing things. The Consequence system, as explained above, refutes inherent existence (*rang bzhin gyis grub pa, svabhāva-siddhi*). Hopkins lists sixteen other names that Consequentialists use for the subtle self that is the object of negation, among which we find:[45]

1) true existence (*bden par yod pa, satya-sat*)
2) ultimate existence (*don dam par yod pa, paramārtha-siddhi*)
3) existence by way of its own character (*rang gi mtshan nyid kyis grub pa, svalakṣaṇa-siddhi*)

4) substantial existence (*rdzas yod, dravya-sat*)
5) existence from the object's side (*rang ngos nas grub pa, svarūpa-siddhi*)

While the various tenet systems disagree about the meaning of these terms, defining, asserting, and refuting their referents in various combinations,[46] the Consequentialists regard them as equivalents and refute all of them both conventionally and ultimately.

The Autonomists refute true existence (something's being its own final mode of subsistence) and ultimate existence (something's being findable under ultimate analysis), but hold that, in conventional terms, phenomena do exist by way of their character, inherently, and from their own side. As seen by Gelukpas, the Autonomy system (and all the systems below it) are unable to separate inherent existence (*rang bzhin gyis grub pa, svabhāva-siddhi*) from existence (*yod pa, bhava*). Autonomists feel that if one were utterly to deny existence from the object's own side even conventionally, then it would be impossible to posit the object at all. There would be no persons, no path, no ethics, no buddha. Thus, while denying that phenomena are findable under ultimate analysis, they assert inherent existence at the conventional level in order to avoid nihilism.

For example, Bhāvaviveka holds that while there is no ultimately existent person, in conventional terms the mental consciousness is the self or person. In fact, most of the lower systems likewise assert that while a person does not exist substantially and is only imputed to the aggregates, there must be something in or among those aggregates (e.g., the continuum of mental consciousnesses, the mind-basis-of-all, etc.) that *is* the person. Imputedly existent phenomena are those that appear to the mind in dependence upon the appearance of something else of a different character. For example, an army appears in dependence upon soldiers, a forest appears in dependence upon trees, a person appears in dependence upon the aggregates of mind and body. In the Autonomy system and below, the imputed phenomenon can always be identified as something in or among its bases of imputation: an army is a collection of soldiers; a person is the composite of the aggregates, or the mental consciousness, or the continuum of mental consciousnesses, etc. From Bhāvaviveka's viewpoint, everything that exists can be found among its bases of designation (and is therefore inherently existent in conventional terms), but cannot be found as its own final nature (and is therefore not ultimately existent).

For the Consequentialists, the so-called "conventional existence" or even "imputed existence" of these lower systems is really a disguised form of substantial existence, i.e., inherent existence. If one can find something that *is* the person among the bases of designation of the person, then this is an analytically findable, ultimately and inherently existent person. When Consequentialists say that all phenomena are merely imputedly existent, they mean that they are not findable under analysis and thus do not exist among their bases of designation even conventionally. The yogi searching for the real nature of the person in analytical meditation does not come up with anything that is the person; he or she realizes only emptiness. Emptiness is, therefore, the final nature, the ultimate reality, the mode of being, of all that exists.

To the Consequentialists, it is a contradiction for Autonomists to assert inherent existence while denying ultimate existence. They argue that if something were in any way to exist from its own side, on its own power, then it would have to be findable under ultimate analysis, and thus it would ultimately exist. The Consequentialists assert that the proponents of other systems (as well as ordinary persons) fail to distinguish inherent existence and existence. They believe that it is possible for the yogi to separate them, refuting inherent existence while preserving the conventional relationships between actions and their moral effects.

Mind Creates the World

That cars and tables are devoid of any trace of analytically findable nature does not mean that they do not exist. Clearly, they do exist. But what kind of existence can things have when they have no shred of existence from their own side?

Like other Buddhists, Consequentialists says that things are "dependent arisings." They exist interdependently, relationally, as part of a matrix of conditions. Three types of "interdependence" are usually discussed: (1) Causes and effects depend upon one another, mutually. For example, fire and fuel; neither exists without the other. (2) Parts and wholes depend upon one another; for example, auto parts and automobiles. (3) Subjects and objects depend upon one another; for example, table and the mind apprehending table. In order to appreciate the radical nature of the Consequentialist position, we have to remember that it is this third type of interdependence that is the subtlest and most crucial. Everything exists only as "mere name," "mere designation," mere imputation by thought. Our *fundamental* problem is not that we believe in "partless particles" or an uncaused permanent Being who causes all existence. Such misconceptions are coarser—and in some way derivative of—the basic misconception, the root of cyclic existence. The root of all suffering is the notion that things have their own ontological status—their own way of existing—without being posited through the force of consciousness. This is what it means to cling to "self" or "inherent nature" according to the Consequence system.[47]

This is quite difficult to understand, and genuinely quite different from the way we usually think of the world. Here is how Tsong Khapa explains it:

> Take, for example, the case of an [imaginary] snake [that is mistakenly] ascribed to a rope. If we leave aside how it is imagined from the perspective that apprehends a snake, and try to analyze what the snake itself is like in terms of its own nature, its features cannot be analyzed inasmuch as a snake is simply not present in that object. It is similar with regard to [all] phenomena. Suppose that we leave aside analysis of how they appear—i.e., how they appear to a conventional awareness—and analyze the objects [in and of themselves], asking, "What is the manner of being of these phenomena?" [We find that they] are not established in any way. [Yet ignorance] does not view it in this way; it apprehends each phenomenon as having a manner of being such that it can be understood in and of itself, without being posited through the force of a conventional consciousness.[48]

If we completely leave aside how a rainbow appears to someone looking into the sky, what is the rainbow from its own side? Would we dare say it is a pattern of light? Do light waves constitute a rainbow on their own, apart from the mind of a viewer situated at a certain point? And if we leave aside how light appears to and is understood by the mind, then what is light in and of itself?

It is not that things have some reality of their own which we, unfortunately, cannot ever seem to get at because we cannot step outside ourselves and adopt a "view from nowhere" or a "God's eye view." Rather, in the Consequentialist view, it is that the mind co-creates everything that exists. Nothing exists except as a conceptual imputation. This is true even of emptiness, and even of the mind that does the imputing.

In the Mind Only system, there is no world external to the mind, but here in the Consequence system, it seems (amazingly!) that a fully functioning, external world is completely dependent upon mind for its existence. For example, when a god, a human, and a hungry ghost each look at a bowl of fluid, the god sees nectar, the human sees water, and the ghost see a mixture of pus and blood. Each being correctly perceives the fluid in accordance with their respective sense faculties. In the Mind Only system, the apparent location of three different fluids together in one bowl is a proof that there are no objects external to the mind. But in the Consequentialist view, this example shows that objects have no intrinsic nature of their own; they exist externally, but only in dependence upon the mind. Thus, the Consequentialist claims that the god, the human, and the ghost are all correct in their perceptions because all three fluids can be simultaneously present in the bowl as external objects. Consequentialist claims about what is possible in an external world without inherent existence are indeed very different from our ordinary ideas about what is possible in a concrete, naturally existent, external world.

We usually imagine that the world is already fully there, fully real, independent of our minds, waiting to be revealed. If this is not the case, then how do Consequentialists account for natural processes that seem to occur at time or places (or at levels of scale) unwitnessed by living beings—like the tree falling in the empty woods, or the Big Bang? Some Geluk scholars, when faced with this type of question, refer to the omniscient consciousnesses of the buddhas as the ever-present minds with reference to which any event can be posited. Others are very dissatisfied with this answer. In India, Geshe Palden Dragpa explained to me that we should simply think of "being imputed by thought" as the measure or limit of how real things are.[49] Kensur Yeshe Tubden (Kensur Yeshey Thubden) gives a similar response:

> When we sleep there are many things we do not see which are posited by the mind. Whether phenomena are seen or unseen, they can fulfill the measure of being posited by the mind. It is not essential that a mind be present. For example, a thousand grams makes a kilo of butter. I may have a one-kilo stone by which, on a balance scale, I can ascertain that a particular lump of butter weighs one kilo. Even if the stone is not present, the measure [of the butter as one kilo] is still there. Analogously, even if the mind which is the positor of something is not present [at that time], the measure of positing it is still there, and it is sufficient that the measure of being posited is fulfilled. Thus, even if no one sees the production of a sprout [in a deserted forest] directly, it is still posited by the mind.[50]

Thus, being "posited by the mind" or "imputed by thought" clearly does not mean that a mind has to be specifically or simultaneously present with the object it posits. The "measure of being posited by the mind" is fulfilled even without a specifically identifiable positing mind.

Does there have to be some specific mind which, sooner or later, cognizes an object? Kensur Yeshe Tubden's example of the butter seems to hint there might not have to be a specific mind for every single thing. However, he also says:

> When a thing is established by terms and minds, then this object, for example, is called a "radio" and is thought of as "radio" by the mind. This thought *is not simultaneous with the thing, but occurs after its existence is established.*[51]

Perhaps one could compare this counter-intuitive "retroactive" dependence upon the mind to the case of fuel and fire, the standard examples of how cause and effect are reciprocally dependent. Fuel depends upon fire to be what it is, even though fuel is fuel even before the fire has started. Fire is logically necessary for fuel, even though fuel has to be there first.

Having studied both modern physics and the Middle Way system, Alan Wallace shares his understanding of this problem:

> A common assumption . . . is that if something is merely a conceptual construct, it does not exist in nature; and if something actually participates in physical interactions, it must be independent of our concepts. The centrist view . . . challenges this assumption by suggesting that the entities conceived by scientists do perform the functions attributed to them . . . but they do not exist independently of scientific theorizing. Such entities are brought into existence by the process of conceptual designation: we designate certain experimental phenomena as evidence of energy, quarks, and so on; and as that convention is accepted, the designated entity exists . . . [T]he conceptual designation of an object is retroactive: for example, once electrons have been conceived, they can be said to have existed for many billions of years in the past.[52]

I have also heard Geluk teachers argue that the effort to "pin down" the exact location of imputing mind is a kind of ultimate analysis. Conventionally, the dependence of things upon the mind to which they appear cannot be analyzed and defined as a matter of temporal succession. The dependence of things upon the mind is the measure of how they exist—conventionally or relatively, in relation to the mind—but not ultimately or absolutely, in and of themselves. Just as tables and chairs and chariots and persons do not withstand ultimate analysis, so *the way that things exist conventionally cannot withstand ultimate analysis.* That is, when one searches to see how things exist, one does not at last find some essential, analytically findable way of existing in things called "conventional existence." One finally discovers only their emptiness, their nature of being devoid of any findable pith or substance. "Conventional existence" or "existence in dependence upon the non-defective mind to which it appears" are conventional phrases that point us toward some sort of understanding of how it is that phenomena do exist and function even while being devoid of any type of existence that can be found under analytic scrutiny. However, like the magician who can understand how the illusory elephant exists only because he has seen the stone and knows that it is falsely appearing to be an elephant, we can gain a full understanding of how things exist conventionally only when we have realized their true nature, emptiness.

Conventional Validity

Conceptual imputation is a necessary but not sufficient condition for existence. Phenomena exist as mere imputations by consciousness, but this imputation must occur in relation to an appropriate basis of imputation; thus there is a difference between seeing a face as a face and mistaking a reflection for an actual face. One of the cornerstones of Tsong Khapa's interpretation of the Consequence system is the notion that ordinary, healthy conventional consciousnesses can be valid, i.e., authoritative (*tshad ma, pramāṇa*), despite being tainted by the effects of ignorance. Consider, for example, an eye consciousness directly apprehending a patch of blue. Autonomists and Consequentialists agree that for such a consciousness the blue appears as something that is inherently existent. Unlike the Autonomists, the Consequentialists consider that it is, on this account, mistaken. Nevertheless, Tsong Khapa claims that such an eye consciousness—despite the mistaken appearance of its object as inherently existent—is completely authoritative and incontrovertible regarding the mere existence of blue. While our ordinary sense of existence is mixed up with the meaning of inherent existence, the two can be differentiated via training in logic and meditation.

Thus, in a similar way, it can be established that the conventional elements of the path—ethical cause/effect relationships, compassion, the sentient beings for whom the bodhisattva has compassion, etc.— do exist and are effective. They exist only conventionally, but to exist conventionally is to exist. Because they are devoid of the intrinsic reality that they appear to have, they are compared to dreams, a magician's illusions, mirages, and so forth. They are designated "falsities" (*rdzun pa*). However, unlike the objects that appear in dreams, they do exist and actions taken with regard to them do have consequences. To dream of committing murder is one thing; to commit murder is another. Tsong Khapa sees the compatibility of the two truths—that is, the non-contradiction between conventional phenomena and profound emptiness—as the key to the Middle Way system. In his *Great Exposition of the Stages of the Bodhisattva Path*, he writes:

> The distinguishing feature of the Middle Way [Consequence] system is the admissibility of all the teachings about cyclic existence and nirvāṇa—the agents and objects of production, refutation, proof and so forth—in the absence of even a particle of essential or intrinsic nature.[53]

Geluk Consequentialists admit that in practice the refutation of inherent existence is a morally perilous task and that success is rare and hard-won. If inherent existence seems to be like a hat that is put on and then taken off, leaving the things just as they were, then the yogi is not getting at emptiness. Because existence and inherent existence are thoroughly entangled in ordinary experience, it should at first seem as though one is cutting at the very existence of oneself and the world. Yogis meditating on emptiness may feel as though the whole world is slipping away and that, were they to continue, they would lose themselves altogether. While the advanced yogi may be able to balance and dance on the narrow ridge of the middle way, for the beginner there is no way to escape reifying ignorance without the courage to press to very the precipice of nihilism.

Standing at the precipice, a yogi should sense that he/she will soon catch his/her balance and be able to posit conventional existence. The Dalai Lama has often said that if it seems that one is going to lose either emptiness or the existence of actions and their effects, then one should give up emptiness—because the correct view of emptiness will not undermine cause and effect. With familiarity, understanding of emptiness should deepen and sustain understanding of the interdependent arising of cause and effect; otherwise, one may be slipping into nihilism. One should cultivate the subtlest view of emptiness that one can harmonize with conventionally existent causes and effects. It is better to stay with a coarse view of emptiness than to adopt a view of "emptiness" that obliterates persons, ethics, the path, etc. Motivated by compassion, the Buddha taught the views of the lower tenet systems for the sake of those not yet able to understand the compatibility of conventional existence and emptiness of inherent existence.

The Two Truths

Tsong Khapa's interpretation of the two truths in the Middle Way Consequence system is intended to show how it is possible that conventionalities (concealer-truths) and emptiness (ultimate truth) are compatible. My summary of his explanation will touch on the following points:

(1) The two truths are mutually exclusive and are a dichotomous division of objects of knowledge (*shes bya, jñeya*), i.e., all existents. There is nothing that is both a concealer-truth and an ultimate truth.

(2) The two truths, although mutually exclusive, are a single entity (*ngo bo gcig*) because emptiness (ultimate truth) is a quality possessed by conventional phenomena (concealer-truths). Just as a table, for instance, exists as a single entity with its shape, so it also exists as a single entity with its emptiness of inherent existence.

(3) The term "concealer-truth" indicates that conventional phenomena are truths (*bden pa, satya*) only for the perspective of an ignorant consciousness that conceals reality. In fact, conventional phenomena are not truths, but are falsities (*rdzun pa, mṛṣā*) because they do not exist as they appear.

(4) Nonetheless, both truths are objects found by authoritative sources of knowledge (*tshad ma, pramāṇa*). Concealer-truths are objects found through conventional valid cognition, while ultimate truths are objects found by ultimate valid cognition.

(5) Concealer-truths cannot be divided into real (*yang dag, tathya*) and unreal (*log pa, mithyā*) because they are all unreal and false in the sense that they appear to exist inherently but do not. However, they can be divided into those that are real in relation to a worldly perspective (e.g., water) and those that are unreal in relation to a worldly perspective (e.g., mirages).

(6) Buddhas are omniscient. This means that they simultaneously, explicitly, and without confusion cognize all concealer-truths and all ultimate truths.

Actually, except for (5), all of these points are anticipated in one or more of the systems already presented. According to Gelukpas, the first point is common to all Buddhist tenet systems. Points (2), (3), (4), and (6) appear to be common to at least some presentations of all Great Vehicle tenet systems.

The Basis of Division

Regarding the first point, many non-Gelukpa interpreters of the Middle Way system, in Tibet and in the West, argue that emptiness, ultimate truth, is unknowable. There are a number of passages in Buddhist sūtras and treatises that appear to teach that emptiness cannot be known—including a famous passage from *Engaging in Bodhisattva Deeds* by Śāntideva (a Consequentialist):

> Conventionalities and ultimates:
> These are asserted as the two truths.
> The ultimate is not in the province of awareness.
> Awareness is asserted to be a conventionality.[54]

Geluk interpreters have understood the third line as a gloss on a passage from the *Meeting of the Father and Son Sūtra*, "That which is ultimate is inexpressible, is not an object of knowledge . . ." and have construed it in various ways. Gyeltsap's commentary on Śāntideva, for example, takes the line to mean that emptiness, unlike concealer-truths, does not appear in a dualistic manner to direct perception.[55] This same sūtra is elsewhere quoted by Tsong Khapa and his followers to show that the basis of division of the two truths *is* objects of knowledge, thus indicating that the ultimate truth *can* be known: "Also, objects of knowledge are exhausted within the two, concealer-truths and ultimate truths."[56]

One reasoning behind the view that the ultimate is not an object of knowledge is the following: Emptiness obviously cannot be the object of a conventional mind, since such minds see only concealer-truths. Therefore, if emptiness is known by any mind, it must be known by a mind of ultimate analysis. However, if it were found by a mind of ultimate analysis, it would ultimately exist. Since nothing ultimately exists, there is no mind that can take emptiness as an object. As explained above, Tsong Khapa counters this by arguing that emptiness is found by a mind of ultimate analysis, but does not ultimately exist because it is not found by the mind analyzing it. Analyzing the table, one finds not the table but the table's emptiness. Analyzing the table's emptiness, one finds not the table's emptiness, but the emptiness of the table's emptiness, etc.

Others have argued that since there is no inherently existent distinction between subject and object, there is no way to speak of the ultimate as being known by a mind. At face value, this is a weak argument because all presentations of the Consequence system are made in conventional terms; nothing exists ultimately or inherently. The two truths are distinguished conventionally, and so also subject and object are distinguished conventionally.

A related argument is that the ultimate is not the object of an awareness because it is not experienced as an object by the only mind that knows it directly. As explained above, direct realization of emptiness is completely non-dualistic. Therefore, the mind realizing emptiness does not experience itself as a subject "over here" knowing an object "over there." This helps us to understand how some non-Gelukpa presentations, framing their systems around the actual experience of advanced yogis, play down the subject/object distinction and even describe the ultimate reality as a type of consciousness.

Gelukpas argue that the mind directly realizing emptiness does not notice the distinction between itself and emptiness because it realizes only emptiness, ultimate truth. The distinction between subject and object falls within the realm of conventionalities, and thus it is not noticed or experienced by the ultimate mind. This does not discredit the existence of such a distinction, however. The duality of emptiness as object and the mind realizing emptiness as subject is established by a conventional valid awareness that recalls an earlier direct experience of emptiness.

Finally, Gelukpas rebut the position that emptiness cannot be known by enumerating the consequent absurdities:[57] (1) Śāntideva would contradict himself because his *Compendium of Instructions* cites the sūtra passage stating that the basis of division of the two truths is objects of knowledge. (2) The Buddha must have taught emptiness without knowing it because it is unknowable. (3) Emptiness does not exist because it is unknowable; therefore, all the sūtras and treatises that teach that great sacrifice should be made in order to realize emptiness are wrong. (4) Since emptiness does not exist, everything exists just as it appears; therefore, we have all known the real nature of things through beginningless rebirths and have no need to be liberated.

In short, the Geluk approach is to avoid mystification and paradox as much as possible and to speak to people about emptiness in conventional language, the language we already speak. Because of its utterly non-dualistic character, direct realization of emptiness is a kind of knowing radically different from that with which we are acquainted. Nevertheless, in order to build a system that is coherent in terms of our present experience, and in order to emphasize the accessibility of ultimate realization (even via conceptual inference), Gelukpas speak of emptiness as known and knowable, something that is to be gotten at and understood.

The Relationship between the Two Truths

The relationship between the two truths in the Consequence system (and in other Great Vehicle tenet systems) is that they are different conceptual isolates (*ldog pa tha dad*)—in fact, they are mutually exclusive (*'gal ba*)—within a single entity (*ngo bo gcig*). This does not mean that every ultimate truth is one entity with every concealer-truth; it means that for every phenomenon, there must be an ultimate truth and a concealer-truth existing together at the same time, inseparably bound, but distinct. This is because emptiness (ultimate truth) is a quality possessed by conventional phenomena (concealer-truths). Just as a table, for instance, exists as a single entity with its color, so it also exists as a single entity with its emptiness of inherent existence. Nevertheless, the table is neither its color nor its emptiness, and neither the color of the table nor the emptiness of the table is the table.

The Gelukpas' scriptural source for this interpretation is a passage from the *Sūtra Unravelling the Thought*:

> The character of compositional phenomena and the character
> Of the ultimate are free from being one or different.[58]

This statement occurs in the context of several examples of "not being one or different," such as a white conch shell and its color, gold and its yellowness, pepper and its hot taste, cotton and its softness, etc. Thus, not being one means not being exactly the same; not being different means being inseparable.

To say that the two truths are different conceptual isolates is to make only the most minimal distinction. When language is present, conceptual consciousnesses tend to flow along the lines of language, and thus two different names imply two different conceptual isolates. For example, "the Fourteenth Dalai Lama" and "Tenzin Gyatso" are different conceptual isolates, even though they are two names for the same person. Actually, Gelukpas make a much stronger distinction between the two truths. They argue that the two truths are contradictories (*'gal ba*), i.e., mutually exclusive phenomena that exhaust all possibilities. Ultimate truths exist as they appear; they are non-deceptive (*mi slu ba*). Concealer-truths are actually devoid of inherent existence, but appear as though they were inherently existent; they are deceptive. Everything that exists must be either deceptive or non-deceptive, and thus everything must be one or the other of the two truths, while nothing can be both. Since the deceptive and the non-deceptive completely exclude one another, the two truths are mutually exclusive.

At the same time, the two truths must be one entity, for if they were not then the emptiness of inherent existence of a table would not be the very nature of the table. Table, lacking a nature of emptiness, would actually be inherently existent. Scriptural support for the oneness of entity between the two truths includes Nāgārjuna's *Essay on the Mind of Enlightenment*, which says:

> Suchness is not observed
> As different from conventionalities,
> Because conventionalities are explained as emptiness
> And just emptiness is conventionalities:
> It being definite that without one, the other does not occur,
> Like product and impermanent thing.[59]

There is also the famous passage from the *Heart Sūtra*:

> Form is emptiness; emptiness is form. Apart from form there is no emptiness; apart from emptiness there is no form.[60]

According to Gelukpa readings, these passages teach the oneness of entity between the two truths; they do not teach that the two truths are precisely identical (*gcig, eka*) or equivalent (*don gcig, ekārtha*). If the two truths were just two names for exactly the same thing, if form were not only empty (*stong pa*) of inherent existence but actually an emptiness (*stong pa nyid*) itself, then merely looking at a form would be enough to constitute realization of the ultimate reality. Since we have been seeing forms beginninglessly, then, if form were the ultimate reality, we should already be enlightened beings. There would be no need for meditation practice, no path, no need for Buddhism, etc. Since this is absurd, Gelukpas emphasize that the oneness of the two truths is a oneness of entity, not an exact identity or equivalence.

On the other hand, as described above, the sense of incompatibility between the two truths diminishes as one advances on the path. A deepening understanding of how things exist conventionally leads one into reflection on emptiness, and vice versa. Thus, in the experience of advanced yogis, the two truths begin to seem like equivalents (e.g., product and impermanent thing), in the sense that realization of one promotes and nourishes realization of the other.

The Terms "Concealer-truth" and "Ultimate Truth"

The term "concealer-truth" (*kun rdzob bden pa, saṃvṛti-satya*) indicates that conventional phenomena are truths (*bden pa, satya*) only for the perspective of an ignorant consciousness that conceals reality, i.e., an ignorant conception of phenomena as inherently existent. In fact, conventional phenomena are not truths at all, but are falsities (*rdzun pa, mṛṣā*) because they do not exist as they appear. They deceptively appear to exist inherently while in fact they are empty of inherent existence.

In his *Clear Words,* Candrakīrti explains three meanings for the term *saṃvṛti:*[61] It may mean (1) that which conceals or obstructs, (2) the relative or interdependent, and (3) worldly conventions. All three of these connotations obtain in various contexts, but in the Consequence system, when interpreting the term *saṃvṛti-satya,* the first meaning takes priority. For example, Candrakīrti's *Commentary on the Supplement* says:

> That through which sentient beings are obscured from seeing things as they are is called an obscurer—an ignorance. This [ignorance], which has the quality of blocking perception of the [final] nature . . . is the concealer (*kun rdzob, saṃvṛti*). Those [phenomena] which, through the concealing [ignorance], appear to be truths . . . are truths for a worldly, erroneous concealer.[62]

Accordingly, as translations of the term *saṃvṛti-satya,* "concealer-truth" or "truth-for-a-concealer" are more precise than acceptable equivalents such as "conventional truth" or "relative truth."

The term "ultimate truth" (*don dam bden pa, paramārtha-satya*) might be more literally translated as "ultimate object truth." According to Candrakīrti's *Clear Words,* each of the three parts of the term refers to emptiness.[63] Emptiness is the ultimate (*dam, parama*) in that it is the final nature of phenomena, their actual way of existing; it is an object (*don, artha*) because it is the object of a wisdom consciousness, and it is a truth (*bden pa, satya*) because it exists as it appears.

Definitions

Gelukpa definitions of the two truths in the Consequence system usually represent the two truths as objects of two different types of valid cognition (*tshad ma, pramāṇa*). Concealer-truths are objects found through conventional valid cognition, while ultimate truths are objects found by ultimate valid cognition. Tsong Khapa's *Illumination of the Thought* says:

> An object found by a reasoning consciousness perceiving, i.e., comprehending, the meaning of reality is a suchness, an ultimate truth. That found by a conventional valid cognizer perceiving a false object of knowledge is a concealer-truth.[64]

Each valid cognizer operates within its own sphere of objects, certifying those objects as existent without damaging the existence of objects in the other sphere. Among sentient beings, conventional valid cognizers are always mistaken consciousnesses because their objects deceptively appear to be inherently existent. Nevertheless, they are authoritative, incontrovertible knowers of their main objects.

In meditative equipoise on emptiness, all conventional phenomena utterly vanish. However, this does not mean that the existence of concealer-truths is refuted by a yogi's ultimate realization. The ultimate valid cognizers of sentient beings are simply unable to realize ordinary phenomena at the same time that they directly realize emptiness. Only a buddha can simultaneously maintain direct cognition of both ultimate truths and conventional truths.

Thus, the two valid cognizers are two different pathways for getting at what exists—like two different wavelengths on a receiver, or listening vs. watching, or glancing vs. staring. One of them, ultimate valid cognition, gets at the way things really are, the final mode of abiding of things—but cannot see persons, actions and their effects, or other phenomena that do not exist just as they appear. The other, conventional valid cognition, can see the class of conventional phenomena—existents that falsely appear to be inherently existent—but is unable to get at emptiness.

Jangya gives us slightly more elaborate definitions of the two truths in the Consequence system.[65] A concealer-truth is:

> (1) an object found by a conventional valid cognizer that comprehends an object of knowledge that is a falsity, a deceiving thing, and (2) that with regard to which that valid cognizer becomes a distinguisher of conventionalities.

An ultimate truth is:

> (1) an object found by a valid reasoning consciousness distinguishing the ultimate, and (2) that with regard to which that valid cognizer becomes a valid reasoning consciousness.

These are based on a passage in Tsong Khapa's *Illumination of the Thought* wherein Tsong Khapa reformulated his definitions "in order to include a buddha's way of knowing."[66] The second clause in each definition is added in order to take account of the fact that all of a buddha's consciousnesses know everything. Even a buddha's conventional valid cognizers know emptiness, and even a buddha's reasoning consciousness knows conventionalities. However, a particular omniscient mind is posited as, or becomes, a conventional valid cognizer through knowing a concealer-truth; it becomes an ultimate mind only with regard to emptiness.

There is some disagreement within Geluk ranks as to whether such "exception-including" definitions are really necessary in general expositions of the two truths. Jamyang Shayba has argued that general definitions need not take account of a buddha's unique mode of cognition. For example, a sense-sphere of form (*gzugs kyi skye mched, rupa-ayatana*) is defined as an object of apprehension of an eye consciousness—even though a buddha can apprehend forms even with an ear consciousness, etc.

Divisions of Concealer-truths

As noted above, Autonomists divide concealer-truths into real conventionalities (e.g., pots, faces, water, horses, etc.) and unreal conventionalities (mirages, reflections, illusions, etc.). Tsong Khapa and a succession of later Gelukpa writers have argued that the Autonomist system's assertion that pots and so forth (unlike mirages, etc.) are real conventionalities (*yang dag kun rdzob, tathya-samvrti*) derives from (and thus evidences) its acceptance of inherent existence, while the Consequence system's refusal to assert real conventionalities is linked to its refutation of inherent existence.[67] In order to be real, something must exist as it appears. The Autonomists and the Consequentialists agree that ordinary sense perception apprehends objects as inherently existent, as though they existed from their own side. The Autonomists argue that this appearance of inherent existence to sense conscious-nesses must be correct, for if it were not, sense consciousnesses would not be valid sources of knowledge. Consequentialists hold that ordinary sense consciousnesses are valid even though mistaken, because their mistakenness applies only to the appearance of inherent existence.

Consequentialists, refusing to accept real conventionalities, assert that all concealer-truths are falsities, unrealities, even conventionally. A horse and a magician's illusion that appears as a horse, a face and a reflection of a face: all are unreal because they deceptively appear to be findable among their bases of designation, while in fact they are empty. If a horse existed as it appears conventionally, then a conventional valid cognizer should be able to certify that it exists in accordance with its appearance as inherently existent. This is impossible because ultimate valid cognition utterly refutes inherent existence.

However, this raises a problem. If horse and illusory horse are both unrealities, if they cannot be distinguished as real conventionality and unreal conventionality respectively, then how can they be distinguished at all? In order to avoid an extreme of nihilism, there must be some way to distinguish complete illusions from illusion-like conventional existents. Candrakīrti's *Supplement to the Middle Way* divides concealer-truths into (1) those that are real in relation to the world and (2) those that are unreal in relation to the world. He states:

> Objects realized by the world [and] apprehended
> By the six unimpaired sense powers
> Are true from just [the viewpoint of] the world. The rest
> Are posited as unreal from just [the viewpoint of] the world.[68]

Thus, for Candrakīrti, the criterion for dividing concealer-truths into real and unreal in relation to the world is the absence or presence of some defect, or sensory impairment, in the apprehending awareness. Tsong Khapa's *Illumination of the Thought* explains that in this context, sensory impairment is brought about by a superficial (*'phral*) cause of mistakenness.[69] Superficial causes of mistakenness are adventitious (*glo bur*), non-innate factors which, when present, produce misperception by impairing the physical and/or mental sense powers. Examples from the writings of Candrakīrti and Tsong Khapa include cataracts, jaundice, consumption of poisonous berries, spirit-possession, a mirror held in front of the face, shouting into a canyon (producing an echo that sounds like another voice), mantric spells and special substances that cause illusions to appear, adopting bad tenets, and dreams. When we speak specifically of concealer-truths, those apprehended by consciousnesses impaired by such superficial causes of mistakenness are unreal in relation to the world and those apprehended by consciousnesses not impaired by such are real in relation to the world.

However, when the distinction between real and unreal in relation to the world is discussed more generally, complications arise because there are some misconceptions that can arise under the influence of either deep, innate conditions or temporary, superficial conditions. For example, the acquired (i.e., tenet-study induced) conception of the person as inherently existent is affected by superficial impairment because it arises under the influence of the adventitious circumstance of having been exposed to a defective philosophy. However, the innate conception of the person as inherently existent is a consciousness free from superficial impairment because it arises from a deep cause of mistakenness that has existed beginninglessly. Nevertheless, the conceived objects of these two conceptions are precisely the same. In such cases, where errors caused by superficial impairment overlap with errors caused by deep impairment, how can we determine what is real in relation to the world?

Tsong Khapa explains that the distinction between unreal and real in relation to the world is made on the basis of whether something is or is not subject to invalidation by a worldly consciousness with respect to its existing in accordance with how it appears.[70] In brief, this means that if one can refute something's existing as it appears without relying upon realization of emptiness, then it is unreal in relation to the world. Otherwise, it is real in relation to the world.

What is the worldly consciousness in relation to which concealer-truths are posited as real or unreal in the context of Candrakirti's division of concealer-truths? Most Gelukpas today agree that it must be a conventional valid cognizer not directed toward suchness. For example, Jangya writes:

> Accordingly, since it appears that it is the thought of the Foremost [Tsong Khapa] to posit as "unreal in the perspective of the world" those objects and subjects that a conventional valid cognizer not directed toward emptiness can realize as unreal and to posit as "real in the perspective of the world" those objects and subjects that [a conventional valid cognizer not directed toward suchness] cannot realize as unreal, it is clear that the consciousness to which "worldly perspective" refers must be a single [type of] consciousness that is not directed toward suchness.[71]

The phrase "not directed toward suchness" means that the worldly consciousness is a conventional valid cognizer that is not informed by, or influenced by, or acting in reliance upon, an earlier realization of emptiness in the continuum of that person. Either that person has never realized emptiness, or has realized emptiness but is no longer perceiving phenomena in the context of that realization.

To give a few examples: Although a table is a false, deceptive phenomenon, it is real in relation to the world because one cannot refute its existing as it appears without relying on a realization of emptiness.

A reflection of a face is unreal in relation to the world because any ordinary mature human can understand that it deceptively appears to be a face, when in fact it is not. A permanent self is unreal in relation to the world because one can refute it through training in lower Buddhist tenet systems, without understanding emptiness. An inherently existent self is real in relation to the world because it can be refuted only in reliance upon realization of emptiness.

Thus far, we have discussed two ways that Consequentialists distinguish a face from a reflection of a face: (1) Is the consciousness apprehending it affected by a superficial cause of impairment (e.g., the presence of a mirror)? (2) Is it possible to realize that it does not exist as it appears without relying upon a prior realization of emptiness? A third way to make this distinction is to ask whether the object designated (e.g., a face) is appropriate to (*rung ba*) or correlated with (*rjes su mthun pa*) the basis of designation. A face that is imputed in dependence upon the front of a human head and a face that is imputed in dependence upon a reflected appearance are alike in both being mere imputations by conceptuality. Neither can establish itself as a face from its own side; neither can be found under ultimate analysis; neither exists as a face by way of its own character. On the other hand, there is a conventional appropriateness in designating "face" in dependence upon the features on the front of a human head rather than to the appearance in the mirror. Although Geluk Consequentialists maintain that all phenomena are mere imputations by conceptuality, they do not regard these imputations as arbitrary. Through the effects of karma, objects and situations that are repeatedly imagined tend to arise, in this or a future lifetime. Nevertheless, an ordinary person cannot transform a cat into a dog just by conceptually imputing it as such; if the basis of imputation does not correlate with the object imputed, then the apprehending consciousness is wrong even from a worldly point of view.

Chapter Nine
The Two Truths and the Bodhisattva Path

Understanding a Buddhist tenet system means understanding its assertions about bases (*gzhi*), paths (*lam*), and fruits (*'bras*). In the Middle Way system's description of the bodhisattva path, this means understanding (1) concealer-truths and ultimate truths, (2) the practices of method and wisdom, and (3) the form and truth bodies of a buddha. Although assertions about the two truths have been our focus here, we have tried to note how each system's assertions about the two truths bear upon the paths and their fruits.

Knowing how to posit concealer-truths, i.e., conventionally existent persons, actions and effects, etc., makes it possible to generate compassion and to accumulate merit through practices such as giving, ethics, patience, etc. that are motivated by compassion. If one loses the ability to posit concealer-truths, falling to a nihilistic extreme, one will be drawn into non-virtuous actions and bad rebirths. Although one cannot fully understand what it means to say that actions and their effects are concealer-truths, i.e., "truths only for a concealing ignorance," until after one realizes their emptiness of the inherent existence that they deceptively appear to have, the conviction that conventional phenomena exist and function is needed from the very beginning.

While an ability to posit concealer-truths such as persons, actions and effects, etc. is necessary for achieving merit and a good rebirth, liberation from cyclic existence is impossible without a wisdom consciousness realizing ultimate truth, the emptiness that is the final nature of all phenomena. Thus, a balanced understanding of the two truths allows the bodhisattva to cultivate both merit and wisdom. The two collections of merit and wisdom bear fruit in a buddha's "form body" (forms that appear in this and other worlds to teach others) and "truth body" (a buddha's wisdom consciousness and the emptiness of that wisdom consciousness).

Some may see it as paradoxical or even absurd that bodhisattvas develop great compassion for beings who do not exist from their own side, beings who are only conceptually imputed, but in practice, wisdom and compassion function synergistically. Realization of emptiness supports, strengthens, and works together with compassion and altruism in several ways: (1) By seeing that there is no inherently existent difference between self and other, the yogi undermines his or her self-cherishing sense of "looking out for number one," i.e., that there is a substantially existent self "over here" that needs to be protected and satisfied to the exclusion of and even at the expense of others. (2) Seeing that he/she shares with all beings a fundamental nature of emptiness, the yogi strengthens the deep sense of closeness and relatedness to others that is critical to love and compassion. (3) In order to aspire to attain buddhahood for the sake of all, knowing the great effort and sacrifice that this will require, the yogi needs firm conviction that it is actually possible to become a buddha. This conviction grows out of an understanding that our present very limited capacity to help others is not inherent in our nature—our nature is pure emptiness, which opens up endless possibilities of self-transformation. (4) Finally, when the bodhisattva trains in compassion-motivated practices such as giving, these are purified and qualified as "perfections" through being associated with the bodhisattva's understanding that giver, gift, and activity of giving are all devoid of inherent existence.

Conversely, altruistic aspiration enhances the development of wisdom by providing a very strong and pure motivation to meditate on emptiness. According to the Consequence system, Lesser Vehicle yogis realize the same profound emptiness that bodhisattvas realize, emptiness of inherent existence. However, Lesser Vehicle practitioners, motivated mainly by the wish to achieve liberation for themselves, approach emptiness through only a few reasonings and achieve the solitary, peaceful liberation of *arhats*. Bodhisattvas, on the other hand, seeking to maximize their capacity to help other beings, become expert in vast numbers of ways to approach realization of emptiness. Driven by their intense altruistic feelings, they train in practices of merit and wisdom for countless eons. The vast accumulation of merit thereby amassed empowers the bodhisattva to abandon not only the obstructions to liberation, but the obstructions to omniscience as well.

Notes

Abbreviation:
P: Tibetan Tripiṭaka (Tokyo-Kyoto: Tibetan Tripitaka Research Foundation, 1956).

1. My example is inspired by the comments of contemporary Ch'an Master Sheng-yen: "Just because a person doesn't have any scattered thoughts does not mean that his problems are resolved. If you are interested in a thoughtless state, just ask someone to hit you hard on the back of the head. There are too many people who cannot distinguish between true wisdom and a mere state of peacefulness. If you do not understand this distinction, even if you practice hard, at best you are being foolish." Excerpted from *Faith in Mind* in Deborah Sommer's *Chinese Religion* (New York: Oxford, 1995), 337.

2. *Descent into Laṅkā Sūtra (laṅkāvatārasūtra)* as cited by Gönchok Jikme Wangpo's *Precious Garland of Tenets* (Dharamsala: Shes rig par khang, 1969), translated in Sopa and Hopkins, *Practice and Theory of Tibetan Buddhism* (New York: Grove Press, 1976), 53.

3. For an example of a traditional Tibetan presentation, see Jeffrey Hopkins, *Meditation on Emptiness* (London: Wisdom, 1983), 353-364. For an example of a Western academic presentation, see Paul Williams's *Mahāyāna Buddhism* (New York: Routledge, 1989).

4. The view that there cannot be a fifth system of tenets is based upon Vajragarbha's *Commentary on the Condensation of the Hevajra Tantra (hevajrapiṇḍārthaṭīkā)* which, as cited in Gönchok Jikme Wangpo's *Precious Garland of Tenets* (Dharamsala: Shes rig par khang, 1969), states, "It is not the Subduer's thought that a fourth [vehicle] or a fifth [system of tenets] exists." See Sopa and Hopkins, *Practice and Theory of Tibetan Buddhism*, 66.

5. Oral comment reported by Anne Klein.

6. *Treatise on the Middle Way* (*dbu ma'i bstan bcos, madhyamakaśāstra*), P5224, Vol. 95, ch. 24, vs. 8-9. For a recent translation with philosophical comment by a Western philosopher, see Jay Garfield's *The Fundamental Wisdom of the Middle Way* (New York: Oxford, 1995).

7. *Great Exposition of the Middle Way* (*dbu ma 'jug pa'i mtha' dpyod*) in his *Collected Works*, Vol. 9 (Ta). (New Delhi: Ngawang Gelek Demo, 1972), 520.

8. Vasubandhu's *Abhidharmakośa and Bhāṣya* (Varanasi: Bauddha Bharati, 1972), 6.4. Also, Tibetan translation: *chos mngon pa mdzod kyi bshad pa*. Dharamsala: Council of Cultural and Religious Affairs, 1969. Root text and commentary are respectively P5590 and P5591.

9. Candrakīrti's *Clear Words* (*tshig gsal, prasannapadā*). Sanskrit edition by Louis de la Vallée Poussin, Biblioteca Buddhica IV (Osnabrück: Biblio Verlag, 1970), 492.10. In Tibetan, Dharamsala: Tibetan Publishing House, 1968 and P5260, Vol. 98.

10. Ngawang Palden's *Presentation of the Ultimate and the Conventional in the Four Systems of Tenets* (*grub mtha' bzhi'i lugs kyi kun rdzob dang don dam pa'i rnam bshad pa legs bshad dpyid kyi dpal mo'i glu dbyangs*) (New Delhi: Lama Guru Deva, 1972), 6a, commenting on Candrakīrti's *Clear Words* (*tshig gsal, prasannapadā*).

11. *Presentation of the Ultimate and the Conventional in the Four Systems of Tenets,* folio 13b.

12. Vasubandhu's *Abhidharmakośa and Bhāṣya,* 91.20-92.

13. What follows is based upon my reading of Ngawang Palden's interpretations in his *Presentation of the Ultimate and the Conventional in the Four Systems of Tenets,* folios 6b-7a. Others may read Ngawang Palden differently, and it is certain that many of Ngawang Palden's opinions are not shared by all of the Tibetan monastic colleges; the reader is invited to pursue further analysis of these points.

14. *Presentation of the Ultimate and the Conventional in the Four Systems of Tenets,* folio 7a.

15. Oral teaching of Geshe Palden Dragpa in Delhi, 1985. He has made this same argument to other scholars who have worked with him.

16. See Anne Klein's *Knowledge and Liberation* (Ithaca: Snow Lion, 1986) and Georges Dreyfus's *Recognizing Reality* (Albany: State University of New York Press, 1997).

17. Generally speaking this is true; however, Jamyang Shayba's *Great Exposition of Tenets* (*grub mtha'i rnam bshad*) (Musoorie: Dalama, 1962) allows that some later exponents of Lesser Vehicle systems accepted the Mahāyāna sūtras as the word of Buddha.

18. *Presentation of the Ultimate and the Conventional in the Four Systems of Tenets,* 34; and Geshe Lhundup and Jeffrey Hopkins's *Practice and Theory of Tibetan Buddhism,* 93.

19. See *Knowledge and Liberation,* 117, for a discussion of how experience (everyday experience and meditative experience) seems to contradict the Geluk claim that generic images are permanent.

20. Dharmakīrti's *Commentary on (Dignāga's) "Compendium on Valid Cognition"* (*pramāṇavārttikakārikā*) P5709, Vol 130, 88.3-5. Translation based on Klein's *Knowledge and Liberation,* 71.

21. *Presentation of the Ultimate and the Conventional in the Four Systems of Tenets,* 34.

22. *Knowledge and Liberation,* 31.

23. *Lamp for the Path (bodhipathapradīpa),* P5344, Vol. 103; Atiśa's commentary on his root text is P5343, Vol. 103.

24. *Sūtra Unravelling the Thought (dgongs pa nges par 'grel pa'i mdo, saṃdhinirmocanasūtra).* P774, Vol. 29, tr. by John Powers in *Wisdom of Buddha* (Dharma Publishing, 1995).

25. *Collection of Related Teachings (samyuttanikāya),* 1.39.10-11.

26. *Supplement to (Nāgārjuna's) "Treatise on the Middle Way" (dbu ma la 'jug pa, madhyamakāvatāra).* Dharamsala: Council of Cultural and Religious Affairs, 1968. Also, P5261 and P5262. These lines are ch. 6, vs. 89, lines *a-c.*

27. Citation based upon Joe Bransford Wilson, Jr., *The Meaning of Mind in the Mahāyāna Buddhist Philosophy of Mind-Only (Cittamātra)* (Ann Arbor: University Microfilms, 1986), 206.

28. This story is related in the colophon at the very conclusion of Candrakīrti's *Supplement to the Middle Way.*

29. *Presentation of the Ultimate and the Conventional in the Four Systems of Tenets,* 61.3-4 and Jangya's *Presentation of Tenets* (Varanasi: Pleasure of Elegant Sayings, 1970), 174.

30. Oral teaching of Geshe Palden Dragpa in Delhi, 1985.

31. In his *Precious Garland of Tenets* as translated in Sopa and Hopkins, *Practice and Theory of Tibetan Buddhism,* 113-114.

32. *Presentation of the Ultimate and the Conventional in the Four Systems of Tenets,* 61.2-3 and 61.6-7; Jangya's *Presentation of Tenets,* 174.

33. This and what follows based on Wilson's *The Meaning of Mind in the Mahāyāna Buddhist Philosophy of Mind-Only (Cittamātra),* 280.

34. According to Wilson's *The Meaning of Mind in the Mahāyāna Buddhist Philosophy of Mind-Only (Cittamātra),* 279.

35. *Commentary on the "Supplement to (Nāgārjuna's) 'Treatise on the Middle Way'"* (*dbu ma la 'jug pa rang 'grel, madhyamakāvatārabhāṣya*). Dharamsala: Council of

Cultural and Religious Affairs, 1968, 152.1-3. See also Wilson's *The Meaning of Mind in the Mahāyāna Buddhist Philosophy of Mind-Only (Cittamātra)*, 271.

36. *Great Exposition of Tenets*, as cited and translated by Hopkins in *Meditation on Emptiness* (London: Wisdom, 1983), 451.

37. According to Ngawang Palden's *Presentation of the Ultimate and the Conventional in the Four Systems of Tenets*.

38. To the best of my recollection, the clairvoyant latecomer is my own addition to the traditional story. If I derived this idea from another source, I am no longer aware of it.

39. Ngawang Palden, *Presentation of the Ultimate and the Conventional in the Four Systems of Tenets*, 111.4-5.

40. Cited from the edition and translation by M. David Eckel, *Jñānagarbha's Commentary on the Distinction Between the Two Truths* (Albany: State University of New York Press, 1987), 163.

41. This is according to the traditions of Loseling monastic college and some others. However, Jamyang Shayba is among those who differ.

42. Again, this is according to the traditions of Loseling monastic college. Jamyang Shayba disagrees.

43. Conversely, the Mind Only system can challenge the Autonomy system as follows: In the Sūtra branch of the Autonomy Middle Way system (as in the Sūtra system), objects and subjects are different entities conventionally. This allows objects to exist prior to the consciousnesses apprehending them. For example, the blue table in instant #1 is a condition for the arising, in moment #2, of an eye consciousness apprehending a blue table. However, unlike the Sūtra system, the Sūtra branch of the Autonomy Middle Way system asserts that the objects of direct perception are not truly or ultimately existent. They exist in dependence upon the non-defective consciousnesses to which they appear. The Mind Only proponent sees this as a contradiction: How can an object exist in dependence upon a consciousness that will not see it—in fact, will not even exist—until the next moment? Does the blue table exist in moment #1 or not? If it does exist in moment #1, then does it not have its own mode of subsistence even before a consciousness perceives it? If it does not exist in moment #1, then how can it be perceived by a non-defective consciousness in moment #2? To put the same argument another way: If, in moment #1, a consciousness apprehending the blue table does not yet exist, and if the blue table cannot exist on its own without depending upon such a consciousness, then how can the blue table exist in moment #1?

For some Geluk Consequentialist responses to this type of problem, see the next chapter.

44. Donald S. Lopez, *The Svātantrika-Mādhyamika System of Mahāyāna Buddhism* (Ann Arbor: University Microfilms, 1982), 315-321.

45. *Meditation on Emptiness*, 36.

46. See *Meditation on Emptiness*, 39 and 631-632.

47. Based on Tsong Khapa's *Great Exposition of the Stages of the Bodhisattva Path* (*byang chub lam rim chen mo*) (Amdo: mTsho sngon mi rigs, 1985), 643-644 and 661-662.

48. Tsong Khapa's *Great Exposition of the Stages of the Bodhisattva Path*, 661.

49. Oral teaching of Geshe Palden Dragpa in Delhi, 1985.

50. In Anne Klein's *Path to the Middle* (Albany: State University of New York Press, 1994), 129.

51. In Anne Klein's *Path to the Middle*, 132. Emphasis added.

52. Alan Wallace, *Choosing Reality* (Ithaca: Snow Lion, 1996), 124-125.

53. Tsong Khapa's *Great Exposition of the Stages of the Bodhisattva Path*, 584.

54. *Engaging in Bodhisattva Deeds* (*byang chub sems dpa'i spyod la 'jug pa, bodhisattva-caryāvatāra*), P5272, Vol. 99, 9.2.

55. Gyeltsap's *Explanation of (Śāntideva's) Engaging in the Bodhisattva Deeds* (*byang chub sems dpa'i spyod pa la 'jug pa'i rnam bshad rgyal sras*) (Sarnath: Gelugpa Students Welfare Committee, 1973), 210.12-14.

56. Tsong Khapa's *Illumination of the Thought* (*dgongs pa rab gsal*) (Dharamsala: Shes rig par khang, n.d.), 195.

57. For example, see Kaydrup's *A Dose of Emptiness* (*stong thun chen mo*) (Dharamsala: Shes rig par khang, n.d), 608.3-6. English translation by José Ignacio Cabezón, *A Dose of Emptiness* (Albany: State University of New York Press, 1992).

58. *Sūtra Unravelling the Thought* (*dgongs pa nges par 'grel pa'i mdo, samdhinirmocana-sūtra*), P774, Vol. 29, tr. by John Powers in *Wisdom of Buddha* (Dharma Publishing, 1995). Thanks to John Powers for drawing my attention to this passage.

59. Verses 67b-68 in Nāgārjuna's *Essay on the Mind of Enlightenment* (*byang chub sems kyi 'grel ba, bodhicittavivarana*), P2665 and P2666. See C. Lindtner's translation in *Nagarjuniana* (Copenhagen: Akademisk Forlag, 1982), 205.

60. The *Heart Sūtra* (*bhagavatiprajñāpāramitāhrdayasūtra*), P160. See Donald S. Lopez's *The Heart Sūtra Explained* (Albany: State University of New York Press, 1988).

61. Candrakīrti's *Clear Words* (*tshig gsal, prasannapadā*), Sanskrit edition by Louis de la Vallée Poussin, 492.10.

62. *Commentary on the "Supplement to (Nāgārjuna's) 'Treatise on the Middle Way'"* (*dbu ma la 'jug pa rang 'grel, madhyamakāvatārabhāsya*), 107.5.

63. Candrakīrti's *Clear Words* (*tshig gsal, prasannapadā*), Sanskrit edition by Louis de la Vallée Poussin, 494.1.

64. *Illumination of the Thought* (*dgongs pa rab gsal*), 194.6-195.1.

65. *Presentation of Tenets*, 461.4 and 468.15.

66. *Illumination of the Thought* (*dgongs pa rab gsal*), 507.

67. *Medium Exposition of the Stages of the Bodhisattva Path* (*byang chub lam rim 'bring*) (Dharamsala: Shes rig par khang, n.d.), 461.

68. *Supplement to (Nāgārjuna's) Treatise on the Middle Way* (*dbu ma la 'jug pa, madhyamakāvatāra*), ch. 6, v. 25.

69. *Illumination of the Thought*, 199.4-5.

70. *Illumination of the Thought*, 201.3-4.

71. *Presentation of Tenets*, 464.7-12.

Sources

Atiśa. *Lamp for the Path (bodhipathapradīpa)*. P5344, Vol. 103. Atiśa's commentary on his root text is P5343, Vol. 103.

Buescher, John. *The Buddhist Doctrine of Two Truths in the Vaibhāṣika and Theravāda Systems*. Ann Arbor: University Microfilms, 1982.

Candrakīrti. *Clear Words (tshig gsal, prasannapadā)*. Dharamsala: Tibetan Publishing House, 1968. Also, P5260, Vol. 98. Sanskrit edition by Louis de la Vallée Poussin. Biblioteca Buddhica IV. Osnabrück: Biblio Verlag, 1970.

————. *Commentary on the "Supplement to (Nāgārjuna's) 'Treatise on the Middle Way'"* (*dbu ma la 'jug pa rang 'grel, madhyamakāvatārabhāṣya*). Dharamsala: Council of Cultural and Religious Affairs, 1968. Also, P5263.

————. *Supplement to (Nāgārjuna's) "Treatise on the Middle Way"* (*dbu ma la 'jug pa, madhyamakāvatāra*). Dharamsala: Council of Cultural and Religious Affairs, 1968. Also, P5261 and P5262.

Chauduri, Sukomal. *Analytical Study of the Abhidharmakośa*. Calcutta: Sanskrit College, 1976.

Collection of Related Teachings (samyuttanikāya). Vol. 1 of edition by Leon M. Freer. London: Pali Text Society, 1884; reprinted, 1973.

Descent into Laṅkā Sūtra (saddharmalaṅkāvatārasūtram). Edited by P.L. Vaidya in Buddhist Sanskrit Texts, No. 3. Dharbhanga: Mithila Institute, 1983.

Dharmakīrti. *Commentary on (Dignāga's) "Compendium on Valid Cognition" (pramāṇavārttikakārikā)*. P5709, Vol 130.

Dreyfus, Georges. *Recognizing Reality: Dharmakīrti's Philosophy and Its Tibetan Interpretations*. Albany: State University of New York Press, 1997.

Heart Sūtra. (shes rab snying po, prajñāhṛdaya). P160, Vol. 6. See Donald Lopez's *The Heart Sūtra Explained*. Albany: State University of New York Press, 1988.

Hopkins, Jeffrey. *Emptiness Yoga*. Ithaca: Snow Lion, 1987.

———. *Meditation on Emptiness*. London: Wisdom, 1983.

———. "The Tibetan Genre of Doxography: Structuring a Worldview." In *Tibetan Literature: Studies in Genre*. Edited by José Ignacio Cabezón and Roger R. Jackson. Ithaca: Snow Lion, 1996.

'Jam dbyangs bzhad pa. *Great Exposition of Tenets (grub mtha'i rnam bshad)*. Musoorie: Dalama, 1962.

'Jam dbyangs phyogs lha 'od zer. *Collected Topics of Rva stod (rva stod bsdus grva)*. Dharamsala, India: Library of Tibetan Works and Archives, 1980.

Jñānagarbha. *Discrimination of the Two Truths*. Edited and translated by M.D. Eckel. *Jñānagarbha's Commentary on the Distinction Between the Two Truths*. Albany: State University of New York Press, 1987.

Klein, Anne. *Knowledge and Liberation*. Ithaca: Snow Lion, 1986.

———. *Path to the Middle*. Albany: State University of New York Press, 1994.

La Vallée Poussin, Louis de. "Document d'Abhidharma: les deux, les quartes, les trois vérités," in *Mélanges chinois et bouddhiques*, Vol. V (1937), pp. 159-187.

lCang skya *Presentation of Tenets (grub pa'i mtha'i rnam par bzhag pa gsal bar bshad pa thub bstan lhun po'i mdzes rgyan)*. Varanasi: Pleasure of Elegant Sayings, 1970.

Lopez, Donald S. *The Svātantrika-Mādhyamika System of Mahāyāna Buddhism*. Ann Arbor: University Microfilms, 1982; revised as *A Study of Svātantrika*. Ithaca: Snow Lion, 1987.

mKhas grub. *A Dose of Emptiness (stong thun chen mo)*. Dharamsala: Shes rig par khang, n.d. Tr. by José Ignacio Cabezón in *A Dose of Emptiness*. Albany: State University of New York Press, 1992.

Napper, Elizabeth. *Dependent-Arising and Emptiness*. Boston: Wisdom, 1989.

———. *Mind in Tibetan Buddhism*. Valois, NY: Gabriel/Snow Lion, 1981.

Newland, Guy. *Compassion: A Tibetan Analysis*. London: Wisdom, 1984.

———. *The Two Truths*. Ithaca: Snow Lion, 1992.

Ngag dbang dpal ldan. *Presentation of the Ultimate and the Conventional in the Four Systems of Tenets (grub mtha' bzhi'i lugs kyi kun rdzob dang don dam pa'i rnam bshad pa legs bshad dpyid kyi dpal mo'i glu dbyangs)*. New Delhi: Lama Guru Deva, 1972.

Nāgārjuna. *Essay on the Mind of Enlightenment (byang chub sems kyi 'grel ba, bodhicittavivaraṇa)*. P2665 and P2666. See C. Lindtner's translation and edition in *Nagarjuniana* (Copenhagen: Akademisk Forlag, 1982).

———. *Treatise on the Middle Way (dbu ma'i bstan bcos, madhyamakaśāstra)*. P5224, Vol.95.

Phur bu lcog. *Magical Key to the Path of Reasoning (tshad ma'i gzhung don 'byed pa'i bsdus grva'i rnam bzhag rigs lam 'phrul gyi sde mig)*. Buxa, 1965.

rGyal tshab. *Explanation of (Śāntideva's) 'Engaging in the Bodhisattva Deeds' (byang chub sems dpa'i spyod pa la 'jug pa'i rnam bshad rgyal sras)*. Sarnath: Gelugpa Students Welfare Committee, 1973.

Śāntideva. *Compendium of Instructions (bslab btus, śikṣāsamuccayakārikā)*. P5335, Vol. 102.

———. *Engaging in the Bodhisattva Deeds (byang chub sems dpa'i spyod la 'jug pa, bodhisattvacaryāvatāra)*. P5272, Vol. 99.

Sommer, Deborah, ed. *Chinese Religion*. New York: Oxford University Press, 1995.

Sopa, Geshe Lhundup and Jeffrey Hopkins. *Practice and Theory of Tibetan Buddhism*. New York: Grove Press, 1976.

Sūtra Unravelling the Thought (dgongs pa nges par 'grel pa'i mdo, saṃdhinirmocanasūtra). P774, Vol. 29. Tr. by John Powers in *Wisdom of Buddha* (Dharma Publishing, 1995).

Tsong kha pa. *Great Exposition of the Stages of the Bodhisattva Path (byang chub lam rim chen mo)*. Amdo: mTsho sngon mi rigs, 1985. Also, Dharamsala: Shes rig par khang, n.d. P6001, Vol. 152.

———. *Great Exposition of the Middle Way (dbu ma 'jug pa'i mtha' dpyod)* in *Collected Works*, Vol. 9 (Ta). New Delhi: Ngawang Gelek Demo, 1972.

———. *Illumination of the Thought (dgongs pa rab gsal)*. Dharamsala: Shes rig par khang, n.d. P6143, Vol. 154.

———. *Medium Exposition of the Stages of the Bodhisattva Path (byang chub lam rim 'bring)*. Dharamsala: Shes rig par khang, n.d. P6002, Vol. 152-3.

Tsong kha pa, Kensur Lekden, and Jeffrey Hopkins. *Compassion in Tibetan Buddhism*. Valois, N.Y.: Gabriel/Snow Lion, 1980.

Vasubandhu. *Abhidharmakośa and Bhāṣya*. Varanasi: Bauddha Bharati, 1972. Also, Tibetan translation: *chos mngon pa mdzod kyi bshad pa*. Dharamsala: Council of Cultural and Religious Affairs, 1969. Root text and commentary are respectively P5590 and P5591.

Wallace, B. Alan. *Choosing Reality*. Ithaca: Snow Lion, 1996.

Williams, Paul. *Mahāyāna Buddhism: The Doctrinal Foundations*. New York: Routledge, 1989.

Wilson, Joe Bransford Jr. *The Meaning of Mind in the Mahāyāna Buddhist Philosophy of Mind-Only (Cittamātra)*. Ann Arbor: University Microfilms, 1986.